영어가 넝쿨째

공무원
기출영단어

PREFACE

어휘 공부는 순식간에 되지 않습니다. 반복해서 공부하는 것이 중요합니다. 여러 단어를 한꺼번에 공부하다 보면 처음에는 그 단어들이 헷갈리고 정리가 안되겠지만 매일매일 반복하다 보면 점차 머릿속에 차곡차곡 정리가 되어갈 것입니다. 그러므로 어휘를 정복하는 가장 좋은 방법은 하루에 자신이 약간 벅찬 정도의 양(하루 100단어 정도)을 정해서 잊어버리는 것을 두려워하지 말고 반복해서 읽어보며 암기할 수 있는 만큼 암기하는 것입니다. 완벽하게 1달에 1번을 보기보다는 1달에 2~3회 반복해서 보는 것이 더 중요합니다. 일단 기억이 잠깐이라도 되는 것은 언젠가 반복이 이루어지면서 재생되어 오래도록 수험생 여러분의 것이 될 것입니다.

일반적으로 공부는 130% 이상을 하라는 말이 있습니다. 왜냐하면 실전에서는 본인 실력의 100%를 발휘하기 어렵고 시험의 난이도에 따라서 여러 가지 변수가 있기 때문입니다. 결국 어려워져 가는 현 공무원 시험의 추세에 맞추기 위해서는 수준 높은 공부가 필요합니다. 그러므로 영단어 공부도 어렵지만 포기하지 않고 꾸준히 공부해야 실전 시험의 난이도에 큰 영향을 받지 않고 무리 없이 시험을 치를 수 있을 것입니다.

수험생 여러분의 합격을 기원합니다.

STRUCTURE

빈출단어(기출예문)

15년간 9급 공무원 시험에 출제되어 온 기출 어휘 중 유의미한 빈출단어를 선별하고 기출 구문과 확인문제를 통해 학습할 수 있게 구성하였습니다.

기출단어(영영뜻)

기출 문제에 나온 어휘와 독해 문제를 분석하여 자주 출제되는 어휘를 선별하여 영영사전 풀이를 하여 어휘의 속 뜻까지 심도깊게 접근할 수 있게 하였습니다.

기출숙어

9급 공무원 시험에서 출제빈도가 높은 영어숙어를 정리하여 단어의 뜻만으로 의미를 유추하기 힘든 숙어들도 단기간에 효율적인 학습을 할 수 있게 하였습니다.

CONTENTS

2005년부터 2019년까지 출제 빈도가 높은 기출단어를 선별하여 기출예문과 함께 수록하였습니다. 2회 이상 출제된 단어의 경우 최근 예문을 수록하여 출제 경향을 파악할 수 있습니다.

01

빈출단어
(기출예문)

2018 제1회 지방직 9급, 2016 제1회 지방직 9급, 2015 제1회 지방직 9급, 2014 안전행정부 9급, 2011 법원행정처 9급

accomplish	완수하다, 성취하다, 해내다.

* That being the case, it's a good idea to consider what short-term goals we can accomplish that will eventually lead to accomplishing long-term goals.
  사정이 그렇다면, 결국 장기적인 목표를 달성하게 할 어떤 단기적인 목표를 우리가 달성할 수 있을지를 생각해 보는 것이 좋다.

* The first is reading for information—reading to learn about a trade, or politics, or how to accomplish something.
  첫째는 정보를 얻기 위한 독서로 무역, 정치, 또는 어떤 것을 성취하는 방법을 배우기 위한 것이다.

2017 지방직 9급 추가선발, 2014 사회복지직 9급, 2007 행정자치부 9급

accumulation	축적, 누적, 재산, (대학에서 높은 학위와 낮은 학위를)동시 취득하기

* An increased accumulation of so-called greenhouse gases in the atmosphere and the potentially disastrous climate changes that this increase may bring about
  이른바 대기 속 온실가스라 하는 증가한 축적물 그리고 이것을 야기할지도 모르는 잠재적으로 재앙적인 기후 변화

* The accumulation of private property is a source of happiness.
  사유재산의 축적은 행복의 원천이다.

* Success arises out of the accumulation of advantages.
  성공은 이점의 축적에서 생겨난다.

2011 상반기 지방직 9급

acquisition	습득, 구입[취득]한 것, (기업)인수, 매입

* The language which he speaks is not an individual inheritance, but a social acquisition from the group in which he grows up.
  그가 구사하는 언어는 개인의 유산이 아니라 그가 자라난 집단으로부터 사회적으로 습득한 것이다.

2019 제1차 서울특별시 9급, 2018 인사혁신처

acute 급성의

* Insomnia can be classified as transient, <u>acute</u>, or chronic.
불면증은 일시적이거나 급성이거나 만성적인 것으로 분류된다.

* Severe <u>acute</u> respiratory syndrome(SARS) is a serious form of pneumonia.
중증 급성 호흡기 증후군(SARS) 은 심각한 형태의 폐렴이다.

2017 서울특별시 9급, 2016 인사혁신처 · 제1회 지방직 9급, 2014 안전행정부 · 사회복지직 9급, 2013 안전행정부 · 서울특별시 9급

adapt ~을 적응시키다, 순응시키다, (건물 · 기계 등을 용도에 맞추어) 개조하다, (소설 · 극을) 개작하다, 각색하다

* But research published since the 1960s has challenged this assumption, showing that it is actually a highly dynamic structure, which changes itself in response to new experiences, and <u>adapts</u> to injuries — a phenomenon referred to as neuroplasticity.
하지만 1960년대 이후에 발표된 연구는 이 가정에 이의를 제기했는데, 이 연구는 뇌는 매우 유동적인 구조여서, 새로운 경험에 반응하여 스스로 변화를 하고 부상(상처)에 적응하며 이를 신경가소성이라 불리는 현상이라고 주장했다.

* The two cultures were so utterly disparate that she found it hard to <u>adapt</u> from one to the other.
두 개의 문화는 서로 완전히 달라서 그녀는 하나의 문화로부터 다른 문화로 적응하는 것이 어렵다는 것을 발견했다.

2009 행정안전부 9급

adjunct 부속물, 부가물

* Fortunately, psychologists believe that books can serve as therapeutic tools — or at least as effective <u>adjuncts</u> to professional therapy — to help children come to terms with their parents' divorce.
다행스럽게도, 심리학자들은 책이 아이들이 부모들의 이혼을 받아들이는 법을 배울 수 있도록 돕는 치료상의 도구, 혹은 최소한 전문적인 치료에 효과적인 부속물로 제공될 수 있다는 것을 믿었다.

2017 제1회 서울특별시 9급

adolescent 청소년

* Both <u>adolescents</u> and adults should be cognizant to the risks of second-hand smoking.
청소년들과 성인들은 간접흡연의 위험성에 관해 인식해야 한다.

affect   ~에 영향을 미치다

- In Europe, where biometeorology began and has flourished, it's assumed that ordinary weather <u>affects</u> ordinary human beings in myriad ways.
  생물 기상학이 시작되고 번창한 유럽에서는 보통 날씨가 수많은 방식으로 보통 사람들에게 영향을 미친다고 생각된다.

- The management of Western Electric's Hawthorne plant, located near Chicago, wanted to find out if environmental factors such as lighting could <u>affect</u> worker's productivity and morale.
  시카고 가까이에 위치해 있는 Western Electric의 Hawthorne 공장 관리자는 조명과 같은 환경 요인이 노동자의 생산성과 사기에 영향을 미칠 수 있는지를 알아내고 싶어 했다.

- Their opinion will not <u>affect</u> my decision.
  그들의 의견은 내 결정에 영향을 미치지 않을 것이다.

 Trading has been adversely _____ by the downturn in consumer spending.

🔖 affected

affordable   가격이 알맞은, 입수 가능한, 저렴한

- Today the technology to create the visual component of virtual-reality(VR) experiences is well on its way to becoming widely accessible and <u>affordable</u>.
  오늘날 가상현실(VR) 경험의 시각적 구성요소를 만드는 기술은 널리 접근 가능하고 저렴해지는 중이다.

aggression   공격성, 공격, 침략, 폭력

- Added to this caring cost is the social cost of canine <u>aggression</u>.
  이 유지비에 첨가된 것은 개의 공격성에 대한 사회적 비용이다.

- Social learning theorists offer a different explanation for the counter-aggression exhibited by children who experience <u>aggression</u> in the home.
  사회적 학습 이론가들은 가정에서 폭력을 경험한 아이들이 보이는 반격행동에 대해 다른 설명을 제시한다.

2009 행정안전부 9급

alienate   (사람을) 멀어지게 만들다, 소외감을 느끼게 하다

* Introduced to characters who share their difficulties, children may feel less alienated and thus freer to discuss and resolve their own plight.

  그들의 어려움들을 공유하는 캐릭터들의 도입으로, 아이들은 어쩌면 소외감을 덜 느낄 것이고 따라서 자기 자신들의 곤경에 대해 토론하고 해결하는 것에 더 자유로워 질것이다.

2008 하반기 지방직 9급

alignment   가지런함, (정치적) 지지

* What a woman feels she has been assigned the role of silently listening audience does not mean that a man feels he has consigned her to that role-or that he necessarily likes the rigid alignment either.

  한 여성이 자신이 조용히 듣고만 있는 청취자의 역할을 부여 받았다고 느낀다고 해서 남성이 여성에게 그러한 역할을 맡겼다고 느낀다거나 혹은 남성이 그러한 엄격한 역할배정을 반드시 좋아한다는 것을 의미하지는 않는다.

2017 제1회 지방직 9급, 2017 제2회 서울특별시 9급

allocate   할당하다

* so it makes sense for the brain to allocate them more subjective time.

  그래서 뇌가 더 많은 주관적인 시간을 할당하는 것은 타당하다.

* The idea that justice in allocating access to a university has something to do with the goods that universities properly pursue explain why selling admission is unjust.

  대학 입학에서 할당제도의 정의는 대학들이 올바르게 추구하는 선과 관련이 있다는 생각은 입학 허가를 파는 것이 왜 불공정한지를 설명해 준다.

2015 인사혁신처 9급, 2014 안전행정부 9급

alphabetic   (숫자나 기호가 아닌) 알파벳[자모]으로 된

* The emphasis on decoding, translated mainly as phonemic awareness and knowledge of the alphabetic principle~

  음소 인식과 알파벳 원리에 대한 지식을 번역하는 해독에 대한 강조는~

* Reading is basically decoding since phonemic and alphabetical knowledge is added to the general decoding process.

  읽기는 단순히 음소를 인식하거나 알파벳을 인식하는 것보다는 훨씬 복잡하다.

alternative   대안

* The government is currently trying to find an alternative to garbage disposal to alternative environmental pollution.
  정부는 최근에 환경오염을 막기 위해 음식물 찌꺼기 처리기의 대안을 찾기 위해 노력중이다.
* We try to eliminate all sorts of other alternative explanations.
  우리는 다른 모든 종류의 대체 가능한 설명들을 제거하려고 노력한다.

anabolic   동화작용의

* Due to the widespread use in sports of anabolic steroids, the lords of the game must accept that the very integrity of the game is at stake.
  스포츠에서 근육강화제의 광범위한 복용문제 때문에 그 게임의 주인인 선수들은 바로 그러한 진정성이 위험에 처해 있다는 사실을 받아들여야 한다.

ancestral   조상의, 조상 전래의, 원형을 이루는

* The author of "The Ancestor Within", Michael Le Page, cited the babies with tails as a likely example of atavism, a phenomenon in which ancestral traits suddenly reappear after thousands or even millions of years.
  'The Ancestor Within'의 저자 마이클 세이지는 꼬리를 갖고 태어난 아기들을 조상의 유전적인 특질이 수천 혹은 심지어 수백만 년 후에 갑자기 다시 나타나는 현상인 '격세유전'의 그럴듯한 예로 인용했다.
* Infectious diseases like smallpox, measles, and flu arose as specialized germs of humans, derived by mutations of very similar ancestral germs that had infected animals.
  천연두, 홍역, 독감 같은 전염병들은 동물을 감염시켰던 매우 유사한 조상 세균의 돌연변이로부터 유래하여 인간에게 특화된 세균으로 발달했다.

2005 중앙인사위원회 9급

Antarctica   남극 대륙(=the Antarctic Continent)

- If we don't protect <u>Antarctica</u> from tourism, there may be serious consequences for us all.
  우리가 관광으로부터 남극 대륙을 보호하지 않는다면 우리 모두에게 심각한 결과가 생길지도 모른다.

- Lichen are one of the few kinds of life that can survive in the mountains of <u>Antarctica</u>.
  이끼는 남극 대륙의 산에서 생존할 수 있는 몇몇 종류의 생명체 중 하나다.

2017 인사혁신처

anticipate   예측하다

- The more we try to <u>anticipate</u> these problems, the better we can control them.
  이러한 문제점을 예측하려고 더 많이 노력할수록 우리는 그것들을 더 잘 통제할 수 있다.

2012 행정안전부 9급

antibody   항체

- Relationship between Flu Vaccine and <u>Antibody</u>
  독감백신과 항체의 관계

2008 하반기 지방직 9급

anti-inflammatory   소염제[항염증제]인

- The <u>anti-inflammatory</u> properties of oleocanthal may help explain the reduced incidence of certain cancers, stroke, and heart disease in Mediterraneanpopulations that traditionally use large amounts of olive oil in their diets.
  올레오캔탈의 특징인 항염증은 전통적으로 식사에 많은 양의 올리브를 사용하는 지중해지역 사람들의 일부 암, 뇌졸중 그리고 심장 질환의 발생률 감소에 대해 설명하는데 도움이 될 수 있다.

2014 법원사무직, 2013 안전행정부

appreciate　　감사하다, 감상하다, 높이 평가하다, 올바르게 인식하다

- Sheila is an English teacher whose voice is very husky, but she is one of the very few teachers who I know can control their classes without raising her voice that is an ability which children appreciate highly.
  Sheila는 영어 교사이며 그녀의 목소리는 매우 허스키하다. 그러나 그녀는 어린이들이 높이 평가하는 능력인 목소리를 높이지 않고 수업을 통제할 수 있는 내가 알고 있는 몇 안 되는 교사들 중의 한 명이다.

2015 제1회 지방직 9급, 2014 사회복지직 9급

approximately　　거의(=very nearly), 대략, 약

- To meet the needs, approximately 2,000 people need to donate blood every day to maintain its supplies.
  필요에 맞추려면, 혈액공급을 유지하기 위해 매일 약 2,000명의 사람들이 헌혈을 해야 합니다.
- Then, approximately 65 million years ago, these huge reptiles died out completely.
  그리고 나서 약 6,500만 년 전, 이러한 거대한 파충류들은 완전히 (죽어서) 사라졌다.
- It takes approximately an hour.
  약 1시간 정도 걸려요.

2019 제1회 서울특별시 9급

arbitrary　　임의적인 제멋대로인

- Communal and official recognitions of childhood send are arbitrary and ritualistically barren.
  어린 시절의 끝에 대한 공동체적이고 공식적인 인정은 임의적이며 의례적으로 척박하다.

2014 법원사무직 9급

artery　　동맥, 주요 수로[도로], 간선, 중추

- Those sleeping six hours a night had an 18 percent higher risk of developing blocked arteries than the eight-hour sleepers.
  밤에 6시간 잠자는 여성들은 8시간 잠자는 사람보다 동맥경화에 걸릴 위험성이 18%나 높았다.
- Great arteries that leave the heart carry the blood to smaller and smaller arteries throughout the body.
  심장을 떠난 대동맥은 혈액을 몸 전체에 있는 점점 더 작아지는 동맥으로 운반한다.

2008 상반기 지방직 9급

articulator 　　조음 기관(허 · 입술 · 치아같이 소리를 내는 데 이용되는 입 속 기관), 발음이 또렷한 사람

* It is still important to construct physical models of human <u>articulators</u>.
인간 조음기관의 물리적 모형을 구성하는 것은 여전히 중요하다.

2011 상반기 지방직 9급

ascend 　　오르다, 올라가다

* Even the dreamer himself, Dr. Martin Luther King, Jr., might not have imagined that 40 short years after his murder, we would be planning an inauguration of the first man of African descent to <u>ascend</u> to the presidency.
심지어 몽상가인 마틴 루터 킹 주니어 그 자신조차 그가 살해 된지 겨우 40년 만에 아프리카 혈통의 첫 번째 사람이 대통령직에 오르는 대통령 취임식을 우리가 준비하고 있을 것이라고는 상상하지 않았을 것이다.

2019 지방직 9급, 2019 제2회 서울특별시 9급

aspect 　　양상, 측면, 이미지

* One <u>aspect</u> of leadership is particularly worth noting in this regard.
리더십의 한 측면은 이 점과 관련하여 특히 주목할 가치가 있다.
* Cultural differences in the meaning of work can manifest themselves in other <u>aspects</u> as well.
일의 의미에서의 문화적 차이는 다른 측면에서도 나타날 수 있다.

2014 서울시 9급, 2006 중앙인사위원회

asthma 　　천식

* Including several interviews with the residents who used to mine but now suffer from <u>asthma</u>~
과거에는 채굴을 하곤 했으나 지금은 천식을 앓고 있는 주민들과의 몇몇 인터뷰를 포함하여~

2019 지방직 9급

associate 　　연상하다, 결부짓다.

* If you want to lose thirty pounds in six months, what short-term goals can you <u>associate</u> with losing the smaller increments of weight that will get you there?
만약 당신이 6개월 안에 30파운드를 감량하기를 원한다면, 당신은 어떤 단기적인 목표를 여러분을 거기에 이르게 할 더 작은 무게의 증가량들을 감량하는 것과 연관 지을 수 있는가?

2017 제1회 서울특별시 9급

astronomer   천문학자

* On a bright spring morning 50 years ago, two young <u>astronomers</u> at Bell Laboratories were tuning a 20-foot, horn-shaped antenna pointed toward the sky over New Jersey.
  50년 전 맑은 봄날 아침, 벨연구소에서 두 명의 젊은 천문학자들이 20피트짜리 뿔 모양의 안테나를 뉴저지 상공 하늘을 향해 조준하고 있었다.

2017 인사혁신처

astute   영리한, 약삭빠른

* Part of it, Keltner thinks, is that poor people must often band together to make it through tough times—a process that probably makes them more socially <u>astute</u>.
  이는 아마도 그들을 사회적으로 훨씬 영리하게 만드는 과정일 것이다.

2011 상반기 지방직 9급

atavism   격세 유전

* The author of "The Ancestor Within", Michael Le Page, cited the babies with tails as a likely example of <u>atavism</u>, a phenomenon in which ancestral traits suddenly reappear after thousands or even millions of years.
  'The Ancestor Within'의 저자 마이클 세이지는 꼬리를 갖고 태어난 아기들을 조상의 유전적인 특질이 수천 혹은 심지어 수백만 년 후에 갑자기 다시 나타나는 현상인 격세 유전의 그럴듯한 예로 인용했다.

2019 지방직 9급, 2018 제1회 서울특별시 9급, 2018 제1회 지방직 9급

attempt   시도, 도전

* As a result, the aggressive driver generally commits multiple violations in an <u>attempt</u> to make up time.
  결과적으로 난폭 운전자는 일반적으로 부족한 시간을 보충하기 위해 여러 가지 위반을 저지른다.
* The more they <u>attempted</u> to explain their mistakes, the worse their story sounded.
  그들이 자신들의 실수에 대해서 설명하려고 하면 할수록, 그들의 이야기는 더 안 좋게 들렸다.

audible 잘 들리는

* However, their suspicion is nearly as <u>audible</u> as their pleasure.
  그러나 그들의 의심은 거의 그들이 기뻐하는 만큼이나 들을 수 있다.

* When such a variable moves in the desired direction it triggers visual or <u>audible</u> displays—feedback on equipment such as television sets, gauges, or lights.
  이러한 가변적인 변수가 원하는 방향으로 이동하면 텔레비전 세트, 측정기나 조명과 같은 장치에 시각적 또는 청각적 신호를 유발시킨다.

audience 청중

* His address at the luncheon meeting was such great that the entire <u>audience</u> appeared to support him.
  오찬 회의에서 그의 연설은 너무 훌륭해서 모든 청중들은 그를 지지했다.

authorize 권한을 부여하다

* Some of the newest laws <u>authorize</u> people to appoint a surrogate who can make medical decisions for them when necessary.
  새로운 법안 중 일부는 사람들이 필요할 때 그들을 위해 의학적 결정을 내려 줄 대리인을 임명할 수 있도록 권한을 부여한다.

autism 자폐증

* Defects can be disabling, and become apparent as disorders such as <u>autism</u> and schizophrenia.
  결함들은 불능화 될 수 있고 자폐증이나 정신 분열증과 같은 명백한 장애가 될 수도 있다.

* Later on, when your dad found out about your younger brother's <u>autism</u>.
  당신의 아버지가 당신의 어린 형제의 자폐증에 대해 발견을 했을 때.

aver   (사실이라고) 단언하다, 주장하다

* Bold claims were made by critics of the day who <u>averred</u> that Russian technology wasn't advanced enough to perform such a feat and therefore the project was a fake.
  그 당시의 비판가들에게서는 러시아의 기술이 그런 업적을 수행할 만큼 충분히 발전하지 못하였기 때문에 그 프로젝트는 가짜라고 단언했던 대담한 주장도 나왔다.

avert   피하다

* A faint odor of ammonia or vinegar makes one-week-old infants grimace and <u>avert</u> their heads.
  암모니아 또는 식초의 희미한 냄새도 1주 된 신생아들의 얼굴을 찡그리게 하고 머리를 피하게 만든다.

barren   척박한 황량한

* Communal and official recognitions of childhood send are arbitrary and ritualistically <u>barren</u>.
  어린 시절의 끝에 대한 공동체적이고 공식적인 인정은 임의적이며 의례적으로 척박하다.

baneful   사악한, 유독한, 파멸을 초래하는

* The <u>baneful</u> influence of tobacco
  담배의 파멸을 초래하는 영향력

beguiling   묘한 매력이 있는

* One of the most <u>beguiling</u> aspects of cyberspace is that it offers the ability to connect with others in foreign countries while also providing anonymity.
  사이버 공간의 가장 큰 매력 중 하나는 그것이 익명성을 제공하는 한편 여러 나라에 있는 다른 사람들과의 연결을 가능하게 하는 것이다.

beneficiary   수혜자, (유산)수령인

* Britain, the biggest single beneficiary of the first age of globalization, was unlikely to gain much from its end.
  세계화 제 1시대의 가장 거대한 단일 수혜자였던 영국은 그것의 종말로부터 많은 것을 얻을 것 같지 않았다.

betray   넘겨주다, 배신하다

* Research shows you'll eat less food and take in fewer calories if you eat slowly, so betray yourself at holiday meals.
  만약 당신이 음식을 천천히 먹는다면, 훨씬 덜 먹게 되고 칼로리도 덜 섭취하게 되므로 휴일 식사 시에 속도 조절을 하십시오.

blooper   (사람들 앞에서 범하는 당황스러운) 실수

* Indeed, the bigger the blooper, the better its chance of helping you becomes a better person.
  참으로 실수가 크면 클수록, 그것은 당신을 더 좋은 사람이 되도록 도움을 주는 더욱 좋은 기회가 된다.

cancer   암

* ~Guards against cancer by removing radicals that can damage cells and push them in the direction of uncontrolled growth.
  ~무절제하게 성장하도록 하는 라디칼을 제거함으로써 암이 생기지 않도록 해준다고 한다.
* It is well known that
  vitamin D deficiency can affect one's muscles, bones and immunity and is even associated with cancer.
  비타민 D 결핍은 근육과 뼈, 그리고 면역력에 영향을 줄 수 있고, 심지어 암과도 관련된 것으로 알려져 있다.

canine   개, 개의, 송곳니

* Added to this caring cost is the social cost of canine aggression.
  이 유지비에 첨가된 것은 개의 공격성에 대한 사회적 비용이다.

capital　　　　자본, 자산, 수도, 대문자

- It becomes man's fate to contribute to the growth of the economic system, to amass <u>capital</u>, not for purposes of his own happiness or salvation, but as an end in itself.

  자기 자신의 행복이나 구원의 목적이 아니라 그 자체의 목적으로서 자본을 축적하기 위해 경제 체제의 성장에 기여하는 것이 인간의 운명이 되어 버린 것이다.

- From the moment a girl is born, the family counts her value as <u>capital</u>.

  소녀가 태어나는 순간부터 그 가족은 그녀의 가치를 재산으로 여긴다.

capitalism　　　　자본주의

- In <u>capitalism</u> economic activity, success, and material gains become ends in themselves.

  자본주의 경제 활동에 있어, 성공과 물질적 이익은 그 자체로서 목적이 된다.

- Most economists have tried to reduce business cycles, but Schumpeter believed that constant change was the strength of <u>capitalism</u>.

  대부분의 경제학자들은 경기 순환을 줄이려고 노력해 왔지만 Schumpeter는 끊임없는 변화가 자본주의의 힘이라고 믿었다.

carbon　　　　탄소

- Today Samso isn't just <u>carbon</u>-neutral – it actually produces 10% more clean electricity than it uses.

  오늘날 Samso는 단지 탄소 중립적인 것만은 아니다. – 그것은 그것이 사용하는 것보다 10% 더 깨끗한 전기를 생산한다.

cardinal　　　　가장 중요한

- As a salesman, you should remember that your <u>cardinal</u> rule is to do everything you can to satisfy a customer.

  판매원으로서 당신의 가장 중요한 원칙은 고객을 만족시키기 위해 당신이 할 수 있는 모든 것을 해야 한다는 것임을 기억해야만 합니다.

2010 상반기 지방직 9급

castes   계급

- In India the breakdown of society into <u>castes</u> is based on ancient mythology that emerged in the Indus Valley after 1500 B.C.

  인도에서 카스트제도로 사회의 계급을 세분화하는 것은 B.C. 1500년 후에 나타났던 고대 신화인 인더스 문명에 근거를 둔다.

2014 경찰공무원 · 안전행정부 · 서울특별시, 2011 상반기 지방직 9급

celestial   하늘의, 천체의, 천상의

- Astronomers in those ancient cultures had no telescopes or binoculars, but they had great power in that they could predict the changing seasons, track time, and predict events like eclipses and the risings of certain <u>celestial</u> objects.

  고대 문화의 천문학자들은 망원경이나 쌍안경은 없었지만, 변화하는 계절을 예측할 수 있고, 시간을 추적할 수 있고, 일식이나 하늘에 나타나는 특정한 물체의 출현과 같은 사건을 예측할 수 있었다는 점에서 굉장한 힘을 가지고 있었다.

- Sailors were able to venture farther out using <u>celestial</u> navigations, which used the positions of the stars relative to the movement of the ship for direction.

  선원들은 방향을 위해 배의 움직임에 따른 별의 상대적인 위치를 이용하는 천체의 항해술을 사용하여 더 멀리까지 모험 할 수 있었다.

2018 인사혁신처

chronic   만성의

- Insomnia can be classified as transient, acute, or <u>chronic</u>.

  불면증은 일시적이거나 급성이거나 만성적인 것으로 분류된다.

2012 상반기 지방직 9급

circumscribe   (권리 · 자유 등을) 제한[억제]하다, ~의 둘레에 선을 긋다

- However, in the United States, we draw boundaries around individual and <u>circumscribe</u> their "space".

  그러나 미국에서는, 우리는 개인의 주위에 경계를 세우고 그들의 '공간'을 제한한다.

circumstances 상황, 환경

* Under no circumstances should you not leave here.
  어떤 상황에서도 너는 이곳을 떠나면 안 된다.
* There is one true answer that fits at all times and all circumstances.
  모든 시대와 모든 환경에 맞는 하나의 진정한 답만 있다는 것이다.

claim 권리

* The insects have earned a new claim to fame.
  이 곤충들은 새로운 명성을 얻게 되었다.

clutter (너무 많은 것들을 어수선하게) 채우다[집어넣다], 잡동사니, 어수선함, 혼란

* Over some time, a few items piled here and there grow into mountains of dangerous clutter.
  시간에 걸쳐 몇 개의 물건들을 여기저기에 쌓아두어 위험한 잡동사니의 산이 되었다.
* Worry is a complete waste of time and creates so much clutter in your mind that you cannot think clearly about anything.
  걱정은 완벽한 시간 낭비이며, 어떤 것도 분명하게 생각할 수 없을 정도로 정신을 아주 어지럽힌다.

cohesion 화합, 결합, 응집력

* Globalization promotes social cohesion and economic equality, not to mention economic benefits.
  세계화는 사회 결합과, 경제적 이익은 말할 것도 없는 경제적 평등을 장려한다.

2018 지방직 9급, 2017 서울특별시 9급

commitment 공약, 약속, 언질, 책임, 전념, 위탁, 위임

* Wish I could but I have another <u>commitment</u> today.
  그럴 수 있으면 좋겠지만, 오늘은 다른 약속이 있습니다.

* Even if they have a lot in their head, they have found a method that the many <u>commitments</u> don'.t impede each other, but instead they are brought into a good inner order.
  그들은 그들의 머릿속이 복잡하더라도 많은 책무들이 서로 방해하기는커녕 훌륭한 내적 질서를 이루는 방법을 찾아냈다.

2015 인사혁신처 9급, 2014 법원사무직 9급

common 흔한

* A <u>common</u> but seriously hindering medical condition~
  흔하지만 심각하게 지장을 주는 질병

* Thunderstorms are extremely <u>common</u> in many parts of the world, for example, throughout most of North America.
  폭풍우는 전 세계 각 지역, 예를 들어 북미 전역에서 매우 흔한 일이다.

2013 안전행정부 9급, 2012 행정안전부 9급

complacent (보통 못마땅함) 현실에 안주하는, 자기만족적인

* The winner's <u>complacent</u> smile annoyed some of the members of the audience.
  그 승자의 만족의 미소는 청중구성원들 중 몇몇을 성가시게 만들었다.

2019 국가직 9급

compulsory 의무적인 강제적인

* Schooling is <u>compulsory</u> for all children in the United States.
  미국에서 학교 교육은 모든 연령대에게 의무적이다.

2018 제1회 인사혁신처 9급, 2015 인사혁신처 9급, 2013 안전행정부 9급

conceive   (생각 · 계획 등을) 마음속으로 하다(품다), 임신하다

* We cannot <u>conceive</u> in ourselves the swift uncomplicated urgency of a reptile's instinctive motives, its appetites, fears and hates.

  우리는 식욕, 공포, 증오 같은 파충류의 본능적 동기에서 보이는 빠르고 단순한 긴급성을 우리 안에서 상상할 수 없다.

* We do not have the choice or control to have everything around us relevant or <u>conceived</u> during our time.

  우리는 우리가 살아가는 동안 우리 주변에서 관련되고 생각된 모든 것들을 소유할 선택권이나 통제권은 가지고 있지 않다.

2017 제1회 서울특별시 9급, 2015 서울특별시 9급, 2014 법원사무직 9급

concern   ~에 관계하다(=relate to), ~에 관계가 있다, ~에 관한 것이다, 걱정 시키다 ; 관계, 관심(사), 걱정, 근심

* It is remarkable that even in a man's most private affairs, where one might imagine society has no <u>concern</u>, conscience leads him to act according to the good of this organism outside himself.

  심지어 사회가 관심을 전혀 가지고 있지 않다고 생각되는 인간의 가장 사소한 문제에서도, 양심은 각 개인을 그 자신의 밖에 있는 조직체의 선에 따라 행동하도록 이끌어 준다는 것이 주목할 만하다.

* The status and rights of British nationals living in the EU and of EU nationals living in the UK are a primary <u>concern</u>.

  EU에 살고 있는 영국 국민들의 권리와 지위 그리고 영국에 살고 있는 EU 국민들의 권리와 지위가 주요 관심사이다.

2013 서울특별시, 2006 중앙인사위원회 9급, 2006 서울시 9급

conduct   수행하다, 안내하다

* The Hawthorne experiment was <u>conducted</u> in the late 1920s and early 1930s.

  Hawthorne 실험이 1920년대 후반과 1930년대 초반에 수행되었다.

* According to a study <u>conducted</u> at the end of 1980, the average high school graduate in the United States has a reading vocabulary of 80,000 words, which includes idiomatic expressions and proper names of people and places.

  1980년 말에 행해진 연구에 따르면, 미국의 평균 고등학교 졸업생은 80,000개의 독서 어휘를 가지고 있고, 이는 관용적 표현과 사람과 장소의 고유명이 포함된 것이다.

conscientious   양심적인

* Highly conscientious employees do a series of things better than the rest of us.
양심적인 직원들은 우리보다 일련의 일을 더 잘합니다.

consciousness   의식

* Despite his theoretical difference from the mainstream viewpoint, Moreno's influence in shaping psychological consciousness in the twentieth century was considerable.
주류 견해와 다른 그의 이론적 차이에도 불구하고, 20세기에 심리적 의식을 형성하는데 있어 Moreno의 영향력은 상당했다.

* Often it's not the need for sleep that is occurring but a gradual loss of consciousness.
종종 발생하는 것은 잠에 대한 욕구가 아니라 점진적인 의식의 상실이다.

conservative   보수적인

* To my conservative friends, it is a term of highest endearment, connoting efficiency and good sense.
내 보수적인 친구들에게, 그것은 가장 사랑스러운 말이고 효율성과 양식을 내포한다.

considerably   상당히

* The larger national awards given in most countries are the most influential and have helped considerably to raise public awareness about the fine books being published for young readers.
대부분의 국가에서 주어지는 가장 큰 국가상은 가장 영향력이 있고 어린 독자들을 위해 출판된 좋은 책들에 관한 공공의 인식을 높이는 데 상당한 도움을 주고 있다.

2008 하반기 지방직 9급

consign

(무엇을 없애기 위해 어디에) 놓다[두다], (좋지 않은 상황에) 처하게 만들다, ~에게 ~을 보내다

* What a woman feels she has been assigned the role of silently listening audience does not mean that a man feels he has <u>consigned</u> her to that role—or that he necessarily likesthe rigid alignment either.

  한 여성이 자신이 조용히 듣고만 있는 청취자의 역할을 부여 받았다고 느낀다고 해서, 남성이 여성에게 그러한 역할을 맡겼다고 느낀다거나 혹은 남성이 그러한 엄격한 역할배정을 반드시 좋아한다는 것을 의미하지는 않는다.

2017 인사혁신처

construct

건설하다

* The minister insisted that a bridge be <u>constructed</u> over the river to solve the traffic problem.

  장관은 교통문제를 해결하기 위해 강 위에 다리를 건설해야 한다고 주장했다.

2018 인사혁신처, 2014 법원사무직 9급

content

내용(물), 목차 ; 만족하는

* What children in remote parts of India lack is access to good teachers and exposure to good-quality <u>content</u>.

  인도의 먼 지역에 사는 학생들에게 부족한 것은 좋은 선생님을 만나고 양질의 콘텐츠를 접하는 것이다.

2017 인사혁신처

contribution

공헌

* An award may honor a particular book or an author for a lifetime <u>contribution</u> to the world of children's literature.

  상은 아동 문학 세계에 평생 공헌을 한 작가나 특정한 책에 주어질 수도 있다.

2019 제2회 서울특별시 9급

conversely

역으로

* <u>Conversely</u>, the United States spends 28 percent of all the money spent in the world on education, yet it houses only 4 percent of the school-age population.

  반대로, 미국은 전세계에서 지출되는 모든 돈의 28퍼센트를 교육에 쓰고 있지만, 학령 인구의 4퍼센트만이 거주 하고 있다.

convince
확신시키다, 납득시키다

* Some people are <u>convinced</u> that life is simply a series of problems to be solved.
  몇몇의 사람들은 삶이 단순히 풀려야 할 문제들의 연속이라고 확신한다.

* I was <u>convinced</u> that making pumpkin cake from scratch would be even easier than making cake from a box.
  나는 상자에 든 케이크가루로 만드는 것 보다 처음부터 호박케이크를 만드는 것이 훨씬 더 쉬울 것이라고 확신했다.

convoluted
대단히 난해한

* Tuesday night's season premiere of the TV show seemed to be trying to strike a balance between the show's <u>convoluted</u> mythology and its more human, character-driven dimension.
  화요일 밤 TV 쇼 시즌 첫 방송은 복잡한 신화와 좀 더 인간적인 인물 중심의 관점 사이에서 쇼의 균형을 유지하려고 노력한 것으로 보인다.

cot
아기침대, 간이 침대, 병원 침대

* He suggested a <u>cot</u> be put in his own room, which he would share with the unwanted guest.
  그는 원치 않는 손님과 같이 쓸 그의 방에 간이 침대를 둘 것을 제안했다.

courtesy
공손함, 정중함, (격식을 차리는 상황에서) 예의상 하는 말[행동], 무료의

* The difficulty could have been overcome or might never have arisen if the people involved had just treated one another with common <u>courtesy</u>.
  만약 연루된 사람들이 보통의 예의를 가지고 서로 대했더라면 그 어려움은 극복되거나 어쩌면 일어나지 않았을 수도 있었다.

2019 서울특별시 9급

cozen

속이다, 기만하다

* The beauty of the pearl, winking and glimmering in the light of the little candle, <u>cozened</u> his brain with its beauty.

  작은 양초의 빛에 반짝거리고 빛나는 진주의 아름다움은 그의 뇌를 그것의 아름다움으로 기만하였다.

2018 지방직 9급, 2013 제1회 지방직, 2005 대구시 9급

critical

비평(가)의, 평론의, 비판적인, 위기의, 결정적인, 중요한

* According to legend, at a <u>critical</u> point in the battle a red banner bearing a white cross mysteriously appeared in the sky.

  전설에 의하면, 전쟁의 결정적인 순간에 하얀 십자가가 있는 붉은 깃발이 불가사의하게 하늘에 나타났다고 한다.

* President Bush knows that a coalition is <u>critical</u> for a military response.

  부시 대통령은 연합이 군사적 반응에 대해 비판적이라는 것을 알고 있다.

* Followers are a <u>critical</u> part of the leadership equation, but their role has not always been appreciated.

  따르는 사람들은 리더십 방정식의 중요한 부분이지만, 그들의 역할이 항상 제대로 인식되어 온 것은 아니다.

2017 지방직 9급 추가선발

cultivate

경작하다, 기르다

* Yet the habit of using them needs to be <u>cultivated</u>.

  그러나 그것을 사용하는 습관은 길러져야 한다.

2019 제1회 서울특별시 9급

curious

호기심이 많은, 특이한

* Human nature has many curious traits, but one of the most <u>curious</u> is pride in illness.

  인간의 본성은 많은 특이한 성질이 있지만 가장 특이한 것들 중 하나는 질병에 대한 자부심이다.

deceive 속이다, 현혹시키다, 사기 치다

* No one was <u>deceived</u> by his insincerity and exaggerated claims about the worth of the properties.
아무도 그 상품들의 가치에 관한 그의 불성실과 과장된 주장에 속지 않았다.

define ~을 정의하다, (경계 · 범위를) 한정하다

* In practical terms, it is more precise to <u>define</u> it as "rule by the majority, having respect for the rights of minority groups and individuals."
실질적 의미로, 그것을 '소수 그룹과 개개인의 권리를 존중하는 다수에 의한 통치'라고 정의하면 더욱 명확하다.

* Six subtests <u>define</u> the verbal scale, and five subtests constitute a performance scale.
여섯 개의 하위 검사는 언어적 등급을 명시하고, 다섯 개의 하위 검사는 수행 등급을 나타낸다.

* There'es an oft-cited 1987 study in which fifth graders were given dictionary definitions and asked to write their own sentences using the words <u>defined</u>.
자주 인용되는 1987년 연구가 있는데, 그 연구에서 5학년 학생들은 사전적 정의를 듣고, 정의된 단어를 사용하여 자신의 문장을 만들어 보라고 요청받았다.

definition 정의

* <u>Definitions</u> are especially unhelpful to children.
정의는 특별히 아이들에게 도움이 되지 않는다.

* For me, the <u>definition</u> of an entrepreneur, is someone who can combine innovation and ingenuity with the ability to execute that new idea.
나에게 있어 사업가란, 혁신과 독창성을 새로운 아이디어를 실행하는 능력과 결합할 수 있는 사람이다.

dejected 실의에 빠진, 낙담한

* Don't be <u>dejected</u>, take courage.
낙담 하지 말고 용기를 가져라.

delivery   배달, 발언, 강연, 구출

* Some people take the time to memorize jokes, and they may even have good timing and <u>delivery</u>.
어떤 사람들은 시간을 내서 농담을 암기하고, 심지어 그들은 농담할 수 있는 적기를 찾아 (농담을) 써먹기도 한다.

* It comes with a ten-year guarantee, and <u>delivery</u> is free.
그것은 10년 보증이 수반되며 배달도 무료이다.

denote   조짐을 보여주다[나타내다], 의미하다

* More specifically, the word <u>denotes</u> the processes and machinery by which such negotiation is carried out.
더 구체적으로, 그 단어는 그러한 협상을 수행하는 데에 근거가 되는 과정과 시스템을 의미한다.

deposit   (은행에) 예금하다, (정확하게) ~을 놓다[두다], (자동판매기 등에) (돈을) 넣다 ; 예금(액), 맡김, 보관

* I don't know how to <u>deposit</u> money.
예금하는 방법을 모르겠어요.

* These[Automated teller machines] are computer terminals that people can use to make <u>deposits</u> or withdrawals and transfer funds.
이것들은[현금 자동 입출금기는] 사람들이 입금 혹은 출금, 송금할 때 사용할 수 있는 컴퓨터 단말기이다.

Example You are advised to _____ your valuables in the hotel safe.

📄 deposit

derivative   파생어, 파생물, (보통 못마땅함) 다른 것을 본뜬, 새롭지 않은

* Therefore, they avoid any <u>derivatives</u> from milk such as yogurt, cheese, and butter.
그러므로 그들은 요거트, 치즈, 버터와 같이 우유에서 나온 그 어떤 것 이든지 피한다.

desirability   바람직한, 바람직한 상황

- This belief is strongest regarding the <u>desirability</u> of an undergraduate university degree, or a professional degree such as medicine or law.
  이러한 믿음은 학부 학위 혹은 의대나 법대와 같은 전문적인 학위를 바라는 것에 관하여 가장 강하게 나타납니다.

desolate   황량한, 적막한, (장소가) 너무나 외로운

- Air temperatures of over 130 degrees in summer are common in this <u>desolate</u> island.
  여름에 130도 이상이 넘는 기온은 이 황량한 섬에서는 흔한 것이다.

deteriorating   악화되어가고 있는, 악화 중인

- The company and the union reached a tentative agreement in this year's wage deal as the two sides took the company's <u>deteriorating</u> operating profits seriously amid unfriendly business environments.
  노사는 양쪽 모두 사업 환경이 좋지 않은 가운데 회사의 영업 이익 악화를 심각하게 받아들이면서 올해 임금 협상에서 잠정적인 합의에 도달했다.

determine   밝히다

- The police spent seven months working on the crime case but were never able to <u>determine</u> the identity of the malefactor.
  경찰은 7개월 동안 범죄사건을 조사했지만, 결국 범인의 신원을 밝혀낼 수 없었다.

detest   싫어하다, 혐오하다

- I absolutely <u>detested</u> the idea of staying up late at night.
  나는 밤늦게까지 깨어있는 것을 극도로 싫어했다.

2018 인사혁신처

deprive   박탈하다

* Plants under water for longer than a week are deprived of oxygen and wither and perish.
  일주일 이상을 물속에 있는 식물들은 산소가 부족하여 시들어서 죽게 된다.

2018 서울특별시 9급, 2015 사회복지직 9급

device   장치, 고안(물), 계획, 방책, 책략

* The real potential for positive computing to make a difference in our lives is in the next generation of wearable computing devices.
  우리의 삶을 다르게 만들어 주는 긍정적인 컴퓨터 사용의 실제 잠재력은 몸에 착용하기 적합한 차세대 컴퓨터 장치에 있다.

* Devices that monitor and track your health are becoming more popular among all age populations.
  건강상태를 모니터링하고 추적하는 장치가 모든 연령층에서 인기를 얻고 있다.

2017 인사혁신처

devise   고안하다, 창안하다

* It is easy to devise numerous possible scenarios of future developments, each one, on the face of it, equally likely.
  미래 발전에 가능한 많은 시나리오들을 창안해 내는 것은 쉽고, 겉보기에는 각각의 시나리오가 거의 같아 보인다.

2017 인사혁신처, 2007 국회사무처 9급, 2005 국회사무처 8급

dignity   존엄, 품위, (말씨 · 태도 등의) 엄숙함, 명예

* Mediation also protects your privacy and your dignity because if you are mediating instead of going to court, your case is not in public view.
  만약 당신이 법정에 출두하는 대신에 조정을 하면 당신의 사건이 대중의 시선에 노출되지 않기 때문에, 조정은 또한 당신의 사생활이나 권위를 보호해 주기도 한다.

* Getting on with our day-to-day lives requires a series of civilized masks if we are to maintain our dignity and live in harmony with others.
  만약 우리가 품위를 유지하고 다른 사람들과 조화를 이루는 삶을 유지하기 원한다면, 하루하루의 삶은 우리에게 연속된 문명화된 가면을 필요하게 한다.

discard   폐기하다, 버리다

* Thus, tens of millions of computers, TVs and cell phones are <u>discarded</u> each year.
따라서 수 천만 대의 컴퓨터, TV, 휴대폰들이 매년 버려진다.

discern   구별하다 식별하다

* so they are fully able to <u>discern</u> what concerns their business.
따라서 그들은 그들의 사업에 관련된 것을 완전히 알아차릴 수 있었다.

disciplined   훈련 받은, 잘 통솔된

* She does this because she is both realistic and <u>disciplined</u> enough to know humans run across too many ideas to remember all of them or even most of them.
그녀는 인류가 그것의 전부 혹은 대부분일 지라도 너무 많아서 기억할 수 없는 수 많은 아이디어들을 발견한다는 것을 알 정도로 충분히 현실적이고 잘 훈련 받았기 때문에 그것을 한다.

disclose   폭로하다 밝히다

* Although the actress experienced much turmoil in her career, she never <u>disclosed</u> to anyone that she was unhappy.
비록 그 여배우는 그녀의 사생활에서 많은 혼란을 겪었지만, 그녀는 자신이 불행하다는 것을 누구에게도 털어놓지 않았다.

discouraging   낙담시키는

* The results were <u>discouraging</u>.
그 결과는 낙담스러웠다.

disparate   이질적인, 다른

* The two cultures were so utterly <u>disperate</u> that she found it hard to adapt from one to the other.
두 개의 문화는 서로 완전히 달라서 그녀는 하나의 문화로부터 다른 문화로 적응하는 것이 어렵다는 것을 발견

disparity   격차, 차이

* That <u>disparities</u> between rich and poor are still too great is undeniable.
빈부의 격차가 여전히 크다는 것은 부인할 수가 없다.

dissemination   파종, 보급

* I believe that the cure for these things is partly to be sought in the deliberate control of the currency and of credit by a central institution, and partly in the collection and <u>dissemination</u> of data relating to the business situation including the full publicity, by law if necessary, of all business facts which it is useful to know.
나는 이와 같은 것에 대한 치유책은 중앙 기구가 통화와 신용 등에 대한 계획적인 통제를 부분적으로 추구하고, 필요하다면 법에 따라 알면 유용한 모든 사업에 관한 사실들에 대해 대중이 완전히 관심을 가지는 것을 포함하여, 사업 상황 관련 자료의 수집과 보급을 부분적으로 모색하는 것이라고 생각한다.

distinctive   독특한, 특유의

* <u>distinctive</u> features of various professions
다양한 전문직종의 고유한 특징

distraction   정신 산란, 주의 산만, 심란

* For example, by escaping into another office, and not allowing any <u>distractions</u> to get in the way.
예를 들어, 다른 사무실로 탈출하여 산만한 상황들에서 벗어나라.

distribution   분배

* Let us examine a situation of simple <u>distribution</u> such as occurs when an animal is killed in a hunt.
한 동물이 사냥에서 죽었을 때 일어나는 단순한 분배 상황을 살펴보자.

disturb   ~을 방해하다, 불안하게 하다, (치안·질서·평화 등을) 어지럽히다

* The boss was <u>disturbed</u> when he saw his employees loafing.
사장은 직원들이 빈둥거리는 것을 보았을 때 불안해졌다.

* Please refrain from smoking in the restaurant, as it <u>disturbs</u> other people.
식당에서는 다른 사람을 방해하므로 흡연을 삼가주십시오.

diversify   (특히 사업체나 회사가 사업을) 다객[다양]화하다, 다양해지다

* With a well-<u>diversified</u> production structure, German and Japanese producers are now more resilient to shocks.
다양화가 잘 된 생산 구조를 가지고 독일과 일본의 제조업자들은 이제 충격에 대해 더 나은 회복력을 갖는다.

doggedly   억세게

* Some people <u>doggedly</u> continue to pursue a goal even after years of frustration and failure.
몇몇의 사람들은 몇 년 후에 좌절과 실패가 있다 하더라도 완강히 목표를 추구하기를 계속한다.

doorknob   (문의) 손잡이

* Say you start to turn a <u>doorknob</u> that has always turned easily.
언제나 쉽게 돌려졌던 문 잡이를 돌리기 시작한다고 말해보자.

edible   식용 가능한

* Allium vegetables — edible bulbs including onions, garlic, and leeks — appear in nearly every cuisine around the globe.
파속 식물들-양파, 마늘, 리크(부추) 등을 포함한 식용 가능한 봉우리들-은 전 세계의 거의 모든 요리에 등장한다.

elaborate   정교한

* You've spilt coffee over a colleague's papers, and immediately you prepare an elaborate excuse.
당신이 동료의 서류에 커피를 쏟으면 즉시 정교한 변명을 준비해야한다.

* The Renaissance kitchen had a definite hierarchy of help who worked together to produce the elaborate banquets.
르네상스 시대 주방에는 정교한 만찬을 만들어내기 위해서 함께 일하는 조력자들의 명확한 위계질서가 있었다.

eligible   자격 있는

* Eligible voters were British, Irish, and Commonwealth citizens (18 and over) living in the UK.
투표의 자격이 있는 사람들은 18세 이상의 영국에서 살고 있는 영국인, 아일랜드인, 영연방 시민들이었다.

eliminate   ~을 제거하다, 삭제하다, 무시하다, 탈락시키다

* I do not mean to suggest that we should seek to eliminate fear altogether from human life.
나는 우리가 두려움을 인간의 삶에서 완전히 제거하려 애써야 한다고 제안하려는 것이 아니다.

* It eliminates the need for the slower phone modems they left back home.
그것은 그들이 집에 놓고 온 느린 전화 모뎀에 대한 필요성을 없애 준다.

* Disorders that people have suffered and died from may now be eliminated.
사람들을 고통 받고 죽게 만들었던 질병들은 이제 사라지게 될지도 모른다.

elongate   길게 늘이다, 길어지다

- scales that were <u>elongated</u> into quill-like forms and that presently branched into the crude beginnings of feathers.

  깃털의 형태로 길어져 나와 곧 깃털의 뭉툭한 끝의 형태로 갈라져 나오는 식의 비늘이다.

emancipate   (법적·정치적·사회적 제약에서) 해방시키다

- The function of the historian is neither to love the past nor to <u>emancipate</u> himself from the past, but to master and understand it as the key to the understanding of the present.

  역사가의 기능은 과거를 사랑하는 것도 그 자신을 과거로부터 해방시키는 것도 아니고, 그것을 현재를 이해하기 위한 열쇠로 통달하고 이해하는 것이다

embossed   양각으로 무늬를 넣은, 돋을새김의

- The African slaves who provided most of the labor that built the White House never imagined that a black man would ever own <u>embossed</u> stationery that read "1600 Pennsylvania Avenue."

  백악관을 짓는 대부분의 노동력을 제공했던 그 당시 아프리카 노예들은 흑인이 '1600 Pennsylvania Avenue(백악관 주소)'라고 돋을새김을 한 편지지를 소유할 것이라고는 전혀 상상하지 못했다.

embrace   포용하다, 수용하다

- When you <u>embrace</u> a portfolio approach, you will be less inclined to dwell on individual losses.

  당신이 포트폴리오 접근법을 수용하게 되면, 당신은 개인적인 손실을 깊게 생각하는 경향이 더 적어질 것이다.

- In fact, perhaps no other country has so fully <u>embraced</u> the Internet.

  사실, 아마도 그 어떤 나라도 그렇게 완전히 인터넷을 받아들이지 않았다.

emigrate   이주하다

- The famine caused another 1.25 million people to <u>emigrate</u>.

  그 기근은 또 다른 125만 명의 사람들이 이민을 가게 만들었다.

2016 서울특별시 9급

encroach
침해하다, 잠식하다

* She was accused of <u>encroaching</u> on the whites—only section, and the bus driver tried to convince her to obey the law.
그녀는 백인 구역을 침범한 것으로 비난을 받았고 버스 기사는 법을 준수하라고 그녀를 설득했다.

2012 상반기 지방직 9급

escalate
확대[증가, 악화] 되다.

* The fighting <u>escalates</u> to a place where you no longer feel like you're understood by your partner.
그 싸움은 네가 더 이상 너의 부모에 의해 이해 받는다고 느끼지 않는 장소에서 확대되어 갔다.

2019 국가직 9급, 2018 인사혁신처

estimate
추정, 추산

* By some <u>estimates</u>, deforestation has resulted in the loss of as much as eighty percent of the natural forests of the world.
약간의 추산에 따르면, 삼림 벌채는 세계의 무려 80%의 자연적인 숲에 대한 손실을 초래해왔다고 한다.

* When giving performance feedback, you should consider the recipient's past performance and your <u>estimate</u> of his or her future potential in designing its frequency, amount, and content.
실행에 대한 피드백을 줄 때 당신은 수취인의 과거 실행과 그것의 빈도, 양, 그리고 내용을 설계할 때 그의 속은 그녀의 미래 잠재성에 대한 평가를 고려해야한다.

2018 서울특별시, 2005 대구시 9급

eternal
영원한, 끝임없는, 불변의

* They believe that material things are transient, while spiritual values are <u>eternal</u>.
그들은 물질적인 것은 일시적이고, 반면에 정신적인 것은 영구적이라고 믿는다.

* Life is really dream, and we human beings are like travelers floating down the <u>eternal</u> river of time, going aboard at a certain point and getting off again at another point in order to make room for others waiting below the river to come aboard.
인생은 정말 백일몽이다. 그리고 우리 인간은 시간이라는 끝없는 강을 따라 표류하는 여행자와 같다. 어느 때에는 배에 타기도 하고 또 다른 때에는 배를 타려고 강 아래에서 기다리는 다른 사람들을 위해 자리를 양보하기 위해 다시 내리기도 하기 때문이다.

euphemism 완곡 어구[표현]

- The usual way of coping with taboo words and notions is to develop euphemisms and circumlocutions.
  금기 시 하는 언어와 관념을 다루는 보통의 방법은 완곡어구와 에둘러 말하기를 전개하는 것이다.

- As old euphemisms fall out of use and new ones come into use, English is ever evolving to handle every situation, pleasant or unpleasant.
  오래된 완곡 어구들이 사용 밖으로 떨어져 나오고 새로운 것들이 사용 안으로 들어옴에 따라 영어는 유쾌하거나 혹은 불쾌한 모든 상황을 다루도록 항상 진화하고 있다.

eventually 최후에는, 마침내, 결국(=finally, ultimately, after all, in the end, in the long run, in conclusion)

- Charles Darwin's work on evolution and Gregor Mendel's on the heredity of plants laid the foundations for the science of genetics, which eventually led to the discovery of DNA, which led to genetic engineering, which is now exploding with unimaginable applications.
  Charles Darwin의 진화론이나 Gregor Mendel의 식물의 유전 형질 법칙은 유전 과학의 기초를 설립했고, 그것이 결국은 유전 공학을 이끌어 갈 DNA를 발견하기에 이르렀으며, 유전 공학은 현재 상상할 수 없는 다방면의 응용으로 확장되고 있다.

- These victims of aggressive acts eventually learn via modeling to initiate aggressive interchanges.
  공격적인 행동의 피해자들은 모델링을 통해 결국 공격적인 교환을 착수하도록 배운다.

evolution 전개, (사건 등의) 발전, (종(種) · 기관 등의) 진화(론), (가스 · 열 등의) 방출

- With the process of evolution, man broke in some cattle to labor.
  진화 과정에서 인간은 일을 시키기 위해 몇몇 가축을 길들여 왔다.

- Back in the mid-1970s, an American computer scientist called John Holland hit upon the idea of using the theory of evolution to solve notoriously difficult problems in science.
  1970년대 중반 John Holland라는 미국 컴퓨터 과학자가 진화 이론을 사용해 어렵기로 악명 높은 과학 문제를 푸는 아이디어를 생각해냈다.

evolve

2017 제1회지방직 9급, 2013 안전행정부, 2006 중앙선거관리위원회

진화하다, (이론·의견 등을) 전개하다, 발전시키다, (결론·법칙 등을) 이끌어 내다, 도출하다

* The origin of species said that all living things on earth are have <u>evolved</u> as a result of descent, with modification, from a common ancestor.
  (다윈의) 종의 기원은 지구상의 모든 생명체들은 공동의 한 선조로부터 변이를 거치면서 혈통을 이어받은 결과로 진화되었다고 말했다.

* It is easy to think of reasons why our brain has <u>evolved</u> to work like this
  우리의 뇌가 이와 같이 작동하도록 발달한 이유를 생각하는 것은 쉽다.

exaggerate

2016 인사혁신처 9급, 2016 서울특별시 9급

과장하다, 포장하다

* Some researchers, though, counter that its reputation as a health threat to people is <u>exaggerated</u>.
  몇몇 연구자들은 건강 위험요소로서의 그 악명이 과장되었다고 반박한다.

* Much of our information comes from chroniclers of the time who often <u>exaggerated</u> the facts.
  많은 정보들은 종종 사실을 과장하는 당시의 연대기 작자로부터 나온다.

excavate

2019 지방직 9급

발굴하다

* I came to see these documents as relics of a sensibility now dead and buried, which needed to be <u>excavated</u>.
  나는 이 문서들을 이제 죽어서 묻힌 감성의 유물로서 보게 됐는데, 그것은 발굴될 필요가 있었다.

exclusive

2017 인사혁신처

독보적인

* The Soleil department store outlet in Shanghai would seem to have all the amenities necessary to succeed in modern Chinese retail : luxury brands and an <u>exclusive</u> location.
  상하이에 있는 Soleil 백화점 아울렛은 현대 중국 소매업의 성공에 필요한 모든 시설을 갖춘 것처럼 보인다 : 최고급 명품 브랜드들과 독보적인 위치

exotic 이국적인

* A romance deals with plots and people that are <u>exotic</u>, remote in time or place from the reader, and obviously imaginary.
  로맨스는 시간과 장소에서 독자들로부터 이국적이고 먼, 명백히 상상적인 이야기들과 사람들을 다룬다.

expire 죽다, 만기가 되다

* China should free him for medical care now and not add his name to the rolls of dissidents left to <u>expire</u> in a jail cell.
  중국 당국은 현재 치료를 위해 그를 풀어주어야 하고, 감옥에서 사망하도록 남겨지는 반체제인사 목록에 추가시키지 말아야 한다.

explicable 설명[해명]되는

* According to the passage above, scientists now consider love as something <u>explicable</u>.
  위 글에 따르면, 과학자들은 이제 사랑을 설명되는 것으로 여긴다.

explicit 분명한

* That is, we must formulate <u>explicit</u> theories in order to reach a satisfactory explanation of the facts.
  즉, 우리는 사실들의 만족스러운 설명을 하기 위하여 분명한 이론을 고안해야만 한다.

exquisite 매우 아름다운, 정교한, 강렬한, 예민한

* Paul Scofield gave an <u>exquisite</u> performance.
  폴 스코필드는 매우 아름다운 연기를 펼쳤다.

2016 인사혁신처 9급

falter
비틀거리다, 불안정해지다, 흔들리다

* He acquired a great reputation because he had set high goals and never faltered along the hard road leading to them.

  그는 위대한 명성을 얻었는데 그가 높은 목표를 세우고 그것들을 이끄는 힘든 길을 흔들림 없이 나아갔기 때문이다.

2019 지방직 9급, 2017 제1회 지방직 9급

famine
기근

* The Aswan High Dam has been protected Egypt from the famines of its neighboring countries.

  Aswan High 댐은 이웃 국가들의 기근으로부터 이집트를 보호해 왔다.

2008 하반기 지방직 9급

fantasize
공상하다, 환상을 갖다

* When you are passed over for a promotion or when a coworker who you think is a friend goes to lunch with the manager who is trying to sabotage your project, you probably fantasize about how great life would be if you didn't have to make money for a living.

  당신이 승진의 기회를 놓쳐 버렸거나, 친하다고 생각했던 동료가 당신의 프로젝트를 파괴하려 하는 매니저와 점심을 먹으러 갈 때, 당신은 아마 먹고 살기 위해서 돈을 벌 필요가 없었으면 얼마나 인생이 멋졌을까 하는 상상을 하게 될 것이다.

2010 행정안전부 9급

fart
(특히 소리가 크게 나게) 방귀를 뀌다

* I fart all the time, Doctor Johnson, but they're soundless, and they have no odor.

  존슨 선생님, 저는 항상 방귀를 끼지만 그것들은 소리는 나지 않고 어떤 냄새도 없어요.

2018 제1회 서울특별시 9급

fertile
비옥한, 풍부한

* This can be because of migration, perhaps, because they move to more fertile lands, or because they are displaced on account of war or poverty or disease.

  이것은 아마도 그들이 더 비옥한 땅으로 이주하거나 전쟁, 가난, 질병 때문에 쫓겨나 이주하는 것 때문일 것이다.

fictionalize

(실화를) 소설화[영화화]하다

- We see <u>fictionalized</u> conflicts on television, but we never get the message.
  우리는 텔레비전에서 영화화한 분쟁들을 보지만 메시지를 얻을 순 없다.

flaw

(사물의) 결함

- Albert Einstein's general theory of relativity is about to celebrate its 100th anniversary, and his revolutionary hypothesis has withstood the test of time, despite numerous expert attempts to find <u>flaws</u>.
  앨버트 아이슈타인의 상대성 이론은 곧 100주년이 다가온다. 그리고 그의 혁명적인 가설은 그의 이론에 대한 결함을 찾아내려는 수많은 전문가들의 시도에고 불구하고 시험의 시간을 견뎌 냈다.

flourish

번영하다, 융성하다, (칼·팔 등을) (위협적으로) 휘두르다 ; (칼 등의) 휘두르기, 과시, 융성, 번영

- Knowledge <u>flourishes</u> best in an atmosphere of free discussion ; and in order to direct social policy wisely it is necessary that there should be freedom to criticize existing institutions and to put forward unpopular opinions, no matter how offensive they may be to prevailing attitudes.
  자유 토론의 분위기에서 학문은 최고로 번성한다. 그리고 사회 정책을 현명하게 이끌어 나가기 위해 현 제도를 비판할 수 있고 비대중적인 견해를 주장할 자유는 있어야 한다는 것은 필수적이다. 그들이 보편적인 의견에 아무리 공격적이 될지라도 말이다.

- It may seem improbable that you can make money by selling to people who don't have much, but companies that have actually bothered to try are <u>flourishing</u>.
  당신이 많은 것을 가지지 못한 사람들에게 판매함으로써 돈을 벌 수 있다는 것이 이상할지도 모르지만 실제로 애를 쓰고 노력한 회사들은 번영하였다.

fluctuation

변동

- The only <u>fluctuation</u> would be due to natural environmental factors, such as availability of food, proper temperature, and the like.
  유일한 변동은 음식의 가용성, 적절한 온도 등과 같은 자연적인 환경 요인 때문일 것이다.

2014 사회복지직 9급, 2005 중앙인사위원회 9급, 2005 국회사무처 8급

fragile   깨지기 쉬운, 망가지기 쉬운, (체질이) 허약한

* The only way to protect this <u>fragile</u> and important part of the planet is to stop tourists from traveling to Antarctica.

  지구의 이러한 망가지기 쉽고 중요한 부분을 보호하는 유일한 방법은 관광객들이 남극 대륙으로 여행하는 것을 저지하는 것이다.

* Small and <u>fragile</u>, they were ideal victims for any predator.

  조그맣고 연약한 그들은 어떤 육식 동물들에게나 이상적인 희생자들이었다.

 Be careful with that vase – it's very _____.

🔲 fragile

2008 상반기 지방직 9급

frantic   정신 없이[미친 듯이] 서두르는, (두려움 · 걱정으로) 제정신이 아닌

* Beginning at breakfast with flying globs of oatmeal, spilled juice, and toast that always lands jelly-side down, a day with small children grows into a nightmare of <u>frantic</u> activity, punctuated with shrieks, cries, and hyena-style laugh.

  어린 아이들과의 하루는 떠다니는 오트밀 덩어리, 엎질러진 주스, 항상 젤리 쪽이 아래에 있는 토스트로 아침을 시작하면서 비명소리, 울음소리, 하이에나 같은 웃음소리가 간간이 끼어드는 악몽 같은 광란의 활동이 된다.

2009 행정안전부 9급, 2005 국회사무처 8급

fraud   기만, 사기, 사기 행위, 사기꾼

* The election results were nullified because of voter <u>fraud</u>.

  그 선거 결과는 투표자의 부정 때문에 무효화되었다.

2018 제2회 서울특별시 9급

frightening   무서운

* The idea of clowns <u>frightening</u> people started gaining strength in the United States.

  사람들을 무섭게 하는 광대라는 생각이 미국에서 힘을 얻기 시작했다.

frugality
절약, 검소

- Conserving water is typically a good thing—except when you're penalized for your frugality.

  물 절약은 당신이 물을 절약한 것으로 처벌을 받지만 않는다면 전형적으로 좋은 일이다.

frustration
좌절(감), 실패, 낙담, 욕구 불만

- I say to you today, my friends, that in spite of the difficulties and frustrations of the moment I still have a dream.

  나는 오늘 나의 친구인 여러분에게 이 순간의 어려움과 좌절에도 불구하고 나에게 여전히 꿈이 있다는 것을 말하고자 합니다.

- First love is well hunger to experience that again before you die, if the alternative is going into a sexual frustration or difficulty or boredom in your current relationship.

  만약 성적 좌절이나 현재 결혼 생활에 대한 어려움 또는 지겨움 중의 하나에 처했다면 죽기 전에 다시 한 번 첫사랑을 만나보고 싶다고 아주 간절히 바라는 것입니다.

fulfill
이행하다, 달성하다, 완수하다

- In other cultures, especially collectivistic ones, work may be seen more as fulfilling an obligation to a larger group.

  특히 집단주의 문화권에서는, 일이 더 큰 집단에 대한 의무를 이행하는 것으로 보일 수 있다.

futile
쓸데없는, 헛된, 소용없는

- The campaign to eliminate pollution will prove futile unless it has the understanding and full cooperation of the public.

  공해를 없애기 위한 그 캠페인은 대중들의 이해와 전폭적인 협력이 없다면 소용없는 것이 될 것이다.

genetically
유전(학)적으로, 기원적으로, 발생(론)적으로

* Consumer advocates call for additional testing of crops and mandatory labeling of <u>genetically</u> engineered products.
  소비자 옹호자들은 곡물에 대해 추가적인 실험과 유전자 조작 생산물 표시를 의무화할 것을 요구한다.
* The first theory says that character is formed <u>genetically</u> before birth.
  그 첫 번째 이론(선천성)은 성격이 출생 전에 유전적으로 형성된다고 말한다.

glob
(액체의) 작은 방울, 덩어리, 반고체의 구슬

* Beginning at breakfast with flying <u>globs</u> of oatmeal, spilled juice, and toast that always lands jelly-side down, a day with small children grows into a nightmare of frantic activity, punctuated with shrieks, cries, and hyena-style laugh.
  어린 아이들과의 하루는 떠다니는 오트밀 덩어리, 엎질러진 주스, 항상 젤리 쪽이 아래에 있는 토스트로 아침을 시작하면서 비명소리, 울음소리, 하이에나 같은 웃음소리로 가끔씩 중단되는 악몽 같은 광란의 활동이 된다.

graduate
~에게 학위를 수여하다, ~을 졸업시키다, 졸업하다 ; 졸업생

* According to a study conducted at the end of 1980, the average high school <u>graduate</u> in the United States has a reading vocabulary of 80,000 words, which includes idiomatic expressions and proper names of people and places.
  1980년 말에 행해진 연구에 따르면, 미국의 평균 고등학교 졸업생은 80,000개의 독서 어휘를 가지고 있고, 이는 관용적 표현과 사람과 장소의 고유명이 포함된 것이다.
* This would be amazing enough in itself, but, even more amazing, Thompson <u>graduated</u> that very same year.
  그러나 더욱 놀라운 것은 Thompson이 같은 해에 졸업했다는 것이다.

grit
모래, 투지, 빙판에 모래[소금 등]를 뿌리다

* However, I know you have too much <u>grit</u> to let a thing like this unduly depress you.
  그러나 나는 네가 강한 투지를 지녔기에 이와 같은 일이 너를 지나치게 낙담시키도록 내버려 두지 않는 다는 것을 안다.

guilty   죄책감

* When a child feels <u>guilty</u>~
아이가 죄책감을 느낄 때~

hallway   복도, 통로

* Blankets and sheets that are thrown over tables and chairs to form caves, miniature cars and trucks that race endlessly up and down <u>hallways</u>, and a cat that becomes a caged tiger, imprisoned under the laundry basket
테이블과 의자들 위로 던져진 담요들과 시트를, 끊임 없이 복도를 이리저리 경주하며 다니는 미니어처 자동차와 트럭들, 그리고 세탁바구니 아래에 갇혀 우리 안에 갇힌 호랑이가 되는 고양이

hassle   귀찮은[번거로운] 상황[일], 귀찮을 정도로 따지기

* We don't look at the curfews as another way to <u>hassle</u> juveniles.
우리는 통금시간을 청소년을 괴롭히는 또 다른 방식으로 보지 않는다.

harsh   가혹한, 냉혹한

* He acknowledged that the number of Koreans were forced into labor under <u>harsh</u> conditions in some of the locations during the 1940's.
그는 1940년대 동안 몇몇 지역에서 많은 한국인들이 가혹한 상황 하에서 강제노동에 동원되었음을 인정했다.

hectic   정신없이 바쁜, 빡빡한

* As mothers, students, caretakers, and professionals, many of us lead <u>hectic</u> lives, filled withboth obvious and subtle stressors that are on our mindsas we attempt to settle into sleep.
엄마로서, 학생으로서, 돌보는 사람으로서, 그리고 전문가로서 몹시 바쁜 삶을 영위하는 우리의 대부분은 잠들기 위해 시도할 때 마음속에 명백하고 미묘한 스트레스들이 가득 채워진다.

hermaphroditically   자웅동체, 암수 한 몸의 ; 상반된 두 성질을 가진

* Under stress, some female lizards that are alive today reproduce <u>hermaphroditically</u>, that is, all by themselves.
  스트레스를 받으며 오늘날까지 살아있는 몇몇 암컷 도마뱀들은자웅동체 즉, 그들만의 힘으로 번식한다.

high−placed   (산꼭대기의) 신전, 제단, 예배소, 중요한 직위, 고관

* Hundreds of Indonesian and Malaysian companies−mostly large agricultural concerns, and some with <u>high−placed</u> Government connections−are using fire as a cheap and illegal means of land − clearing.
  대게는 농업적 관심사가 크고, 몇몇은 고위직을 가진 정부 관련자들의 수백의 인도네시아와 말레이시아 회사들은 싸고 불법적인 개간의 수단으로 불을 사용한다.

hospitable   (기후, 환경이) 쾌적한

* But that has not happened, leading researchers to think that the more northern habitats may be less <u>hospitable</u> to them.
  그러나 그러한 일은 일어나지 않았고, 연구자들은 보다 북쪽의 서식지가 호박벌들에게 덜 쾌적할 수 있다고 생각하게 되었다.

hospitality   친절, 환대

* However, such a refusal is often viewed as a rejection of someone's <u>hospitality</u> and thoughtlessness in other cultures, particularly when no is made for the refusal.
  그러나 그러한 거절이 다른 문화에서는 누군가의 친절에 대한 거절로, 그리고 인정이 없는 걸로 종종 여겨진다. 특히나 그 거절에 대한 어떠한 변명도 없을 때는 더 그렇다.

hostile
적(국)의, 적의가 있는, (~에) 반대하는, 적대적인

* The mental world of the ordinary man consists of beliefs which he has accepted without questioning and to which he is firmly attached ; he is instinctively <u>hostile</u> to anything which would upset the established order of this familiar world.

  평범한 사람의 정신세계는 그가 의심 없이 받아들이고 확고하게 애착을 가지고 있는 믿음들로 구성되어 있다. 그래서 그는 본능적으로 익숙한 세계의 기존 질서를 망치는 것에 대해 적대적이다.

hovered
(허공/수줍거나 자신감 없는 태도로 특히 다른 사람 주위를/무엇의 가까이 · 불확실한, 상태에) 맴돌다, 서성이다

* According to police, the helicopter flew into the prison at about 10:45 A.M. and <u>hovered</u> over a prison building.

  경찰에 의하면, 약 오전 10:45분쯤 그 헬리콥터는 감옥으로 날아들었고 교도소의 상공을 맴돌고 있었다.

humanity
인류, 인간, 인간성, 자비

* Plato ─ who may have understood better what forms the mind of man than do some of our contemporaries who want their children exposed only to "real" people and everyday events ─ knew what intellectual experiences make for true <u>humanity</u>.

  자녀들이 오로지 '진실한' 사람들과 일상적인 사건(행사)에만 노출되기를 원하는 일부 현대인들보다 무엇이 인간의 지성을 형성하는지를 더 잘 이해했을지도 모를 플라톤은 어떠한 지적인 경험이 참된 인간성에 이바지하는지를 알고 있었다.

* He based his personal philosophy on a "reverence for life" and on a deep commitment to serve <u>humanity</u> through thought and action.

  그는 그의 개인 철학의 바탕을 '생명에 대한 존경심' 그리고 생각과 행동을 통해 인류에 봉사하는 깊은 헌신에 두었다.

hygiene
위생

* Roberts owes their success to "<u>hygiene</u>" factors.

  로버츠는 그들의 성공이 "위생"요인 덕분이라고 한다.

hypnoid
최면양(催眠樣)의, 최면모양의

* Like any other kind of <u>hypnoid</u> suggestion, it tries to impress its customers emotionally and then make them submit intellectually.

여타 다른 종류의 최면양의 제안과 같이, 그것은 고객들에게 감정적으로 깊은 인상을 주어 그들이 지성적으로 항복하기를 시도한다.

hyperactive
(특히 아동들이나 그들의 행동이) 활동 과잉의

* Necessities for the early treatment of <u>hyperactive</u> children

과잉 성 행동 아동들을 위한 조기 치료의 필요성

illegible
읽기 어려운, 판독이 불가능한

* <u>Illegible</u> handwriting does not indicate weakness of character, as even a quick glance at the penmanship of George Washington, Franklin D. Roosevelt, or John F. Kennedy reveals.

조지 워싱턴, 프랭클린 루즈벨트 또는 존 케네디의 서법에서 힐끗 볼 수 있듯이 읽기 어려운 필체는 성격의 약점을 나타내지 않는다.

impairment
(신체적 · 정신적) 장애

* And these same factors are also the cause of the unemployment of labor, or the disappointment of reasonable business expectations, and of the <u>impairment</u> of efficiency and production.

그리고 이러한 유사한 요인들 역시 실업 혹은 타당한 사업 기대에 대한 실망, 그리고 효율성과 생산 장애의 원인이 된다.

impart
(정보 · 지식 등을) 전하다, (특정한 특성을) 주다

* I suggest to you that the knowledge the novelist <u>imparts</u> is biased and thus unreliable and it is better not to know a thing at all than to know it in a distorted fashion.

그 소설가가 전하는 지식은 편향되어 믿음직하지 못하기에 그것에 대해 왜곡된 방식으로 아는 것 보다는 전혀 알지 못하는 것이 더 낫다.

impede
방해하다, 지연시키다, 저해하다

* Researchers from a university surveyed more than 3,000 primary school children of all ages and found that 10% of them suffer from poor working memory, which seriously <u>impedes</u> their learning.

  대학의 연구자들은 다양한 연령의 3,000명 이상의 초등학생들을 연구했고 그들 중 10%가 기억력이 좋지 않아 고생을 한다는 것을 밝혀냈는데, 이는 그들의 학습능력을 심각하게 방해했다.

imperceptible
감지할 수 없는

* In any given year such a small increment has probably been <u>imperceptible</u>. But the accumulated increase over two decades is substantial.

  어떤 특정한 해에 그러한 작은 증가는 아마 느껴지지 않을 수 있다. 하지만 지난 20년 동안 축적된 양은 상당하다.

implement
이행하다, 수행하다 ; 수단, 방법, 도구

* Sometimes the work was hard ; the <u>implements</u> had been designed for human beings and not for animals, and it was a great drawback that no animal was able to use any tool that involved standing on his hind legs.

  때때로 일하는 것은 힘들었다. 농구가 동물을 위해서가 아니라 인간을 위해서 설계되었기 때문이다. 그리고 어떤 동물도 뒷다리로 서서 도구를 사용할 수 없다는 것은 커다란 약점이었다.

impressive
인상에 남는, 인상적인, 감동적인, 장엄한

* His reasoning is <u>impressive</u>, but not to the point.

  그의 추리는 인상적이었지만, 적절하지는 못했다.

inaugural
(공식적인 연설 · 모임 등에 대해) 취임(식)의, 개회의, 첫

* His <u>inaugural</u> address was hilarious.

  그의 취임연설은 아주 재미있었다.

2011 상반기 지방직 9급

inauguration
(대통령·교수 등의) 취임(식), (신시대 등의) 개시, (공공시설 등의) 정식 개업, 준공식

* Even the dreamer himself, Dr. Martin Luther King, Jr., might not have imagined that 40 short years after his murder, we would be planning an <u>inauguration</u> of the first man of African descent to ascend to the presidency.
  심지어 몽상가인 마틴 루터 킹 주니어 그 자신조차 그가 살해 된지 겨우 40년 만에 아프리카 혈통의 첫 번째 사람이 대통령직에 오르는 대통령 취임식을 우리가 준비하고 있을 것이라고는 상상하지 않았을 것이다.

2018 제2회 서울특별시 9급

inconvenient
불편한, 곤란한

* Mr. Johnson objected to the proposal because it was founded on a wrong principle and also was <u>inconvenient</u> at times.
  존슨 씨는 그 제안이 잘못된 원칙에 근거하고 있고 때때로 불편하기 때문에 반대했다.

2019 제1회 서울특별시 9급

indicate
나타내다, 보여주다

* Some athletes <u>indicated</u> that negative weight − related comments from family were pivotal events in the development of eating disorders.
  몇몇 운동선수들은 가족으로부터의 체중과 관련된 부정적인 언급이 식이장애의 발달에 있어 중요한 사건이라는 것을 보여주었다.

2018 인사혁신처

indigenous
토착의, 토종의

* Robert J. Flaherty, a legendary documentary filmmaker, tried to show how <u>indigenous</u> people gathered food.
  전설적인 다큐멘터리 영화 제작자인 Robert J. Flaherty는 어떻게 토착민들이 음식을 모았는지를 보여주려고 노력했다.

2017 지방직 9급, 2010 행정안전부 9급

induce　　　　설득하다, 유도하다, 초래하다

* Active euthanasia means that a physician or other medical personnel takes a deliberate action that will induce death.
  적극적 안락사란 내과의사 또는 의료인이 죽음으로 이끄는 계획된 행동을 취하는 것을 의미한다.

* Novelty-induced time expansion is a well-characterized phenomenon which can be investigated under laboratory conditions.
  새로움으로 유도된 시간 확장은 실험실 조건 아래에서 조사될 수 있는 잘 특징지어진 현상이다.

2009 행정안전부 9급

indulge　　　　(특히 좋지 않다고 여겨지는 것을) 마음껏 하다, (특정한 욕구·관심 등을) 충족시키다, ~가 제멋대로 굴게 하다, (특히 불법적인 활동에) 가담하다

* The dangerous man is not the critic, but the noisy empty patriot who encourages us to indulge in orgies of self-congratulation.
  그 위험한 남자는 비평가가 아니고, 우리가 엄청난 자축을 마음껏 하도록 격려하는 시끄럽고 삶이 공허한 애국자였다.

2017 인사혁신처

inequality　　　　불균형, 불평등

* This inequality is corrected by their getting in their turn better portions from kills by other people.
  이러한 불평등은 그들이 다른 사람들의 사냥감으로부터 더 좋은 몫을 받게 됨으로 바로잡을 수 있다.

2012 상반기 지방직 9급

inexplicable　　　　불가해한, 설명할 수 없는

* Romance has seemed as inexplicable as the beauty of a rainbow.
  사랑은 무지개의 아름다움만큼이나 설명할 수 없는 것 같다.

2017 제2회 서울특별시 9급

inextricably　　　　불가분하게, 떼려야 뗄 수 없이

* Leadership and strength are inextricably bound together.
  지도력과 힘은 떼려야 뗄 수 없이 서로 연관되어 있다.

infant   유아, 소아, 갓난아기 ; 유아의

* It's a vital means of communication and the first way that <u>infants</u> establish any kind of control over their lives.

  그것은 의사소통의 필수적인 방법이고 유아가 그들의 삶에 대해 통제력을 확고히 하는 최초의 방법이다.

* A faint odor of ammonia or vinegar makes one-week-old <u>infants</u> grimace and avert their heads.

  암모니아 또는 식초의 희미한 냄새도 1주된 신생아들의 얼굴을 찡그리게 하고 머리를 피하게 만든다.

inflame   흥분[격앙/격분] 시키다, (상황을) 악화시키다

* Should the wound be <u>inflames</u>, call me at once.

  상처에 염증이 나면 즉시 나에게 전화해라.

inflict   (괴로움 등을) 가하다[안기다]

* He got a deadly wound <u>inflicted</u> in the skirmish with the well-trained enemy squad.

  그는 소규모 충돌에서 잘 훈련된 적의 부대에 의해 매우 치명적인 부상을 입었다.

influential   영향력 있는

* The larger national awards given in most countries are the most <u>influential</u> and have helped considerably to raise public awareness about the fine books being published for young readers.

  대부분의 국가에서 주어지는 가장 큰 국가상은 가장 영향력이 있고 어린 독자들을 위해 출판된 좋은 책들에 관한 공공의 인식을 높이는 데 상당한 도움을 주고 있다.

initiate 　　　　　개시되게 하다, 착수시키다

* Acute insomnia is present when there is difficulty initiating or maintaining sleep or when the sleep that is obtained is not refreshing.
  급성 불면증은 잠이 드는 것 혹은 잠을 계속 자는 것에 어려움이 있을 때 혹은 수면이 상쾌하지 않을 때 발생한다.

* These victims of aggressive acts eventually learn via modeling to initiate aggressive interchanges.
  공격적인 행동의 피해자들은 모델링을 통해 결국 공격적인 교환을 착수하도록 배운다.

injection 　　　　　주입, 주사

* Even the death by electrocution and death by injection sound absurd and incongruous with modern society.
  심지어 전기 사형과 주사를 주입하는 사형조차도 현대사회에 불합리하고도 부조리하게 들린다.

injury 　　　　　부상, 상처, 명예 훼손, 손상

* Toy-related injuries for last year are estimated at about two million.
  작년 장난감과 관련된 부상은 어림잡아 약 200만 건이다.

* He is more generous about forgiving a slight, an insult, and an injury.
  그는 경멸과 모욕, 명예 훼손을 용서하는 것에 보다 더 관대하다.

insecure 　　　　　불안정한, 위태로운, 걱정스러운

* As a result, many teenage girls have become insecure about their bodies and obsessed with losing weight.
  결과적으로 많은 십대 소녀들은 자신의 몸매에 대해서 자신 없어 하고, 체중을 감량하느라 괴로워한다.

insistent   계속되는

* Penzias heards the <u>insistent</u> hiss of radio signals coming from every direction
— and from beyond the Milky Way.
Penzias가 – 우리 은하 건너편으로부터, 그리고 모든 방향으로부터 계속되는 전자기파의 소리를 들었다.

inspire   고무하다

* The scientific designs of airplanes were <u>inspired</u> by shark scales.
비행기의 과학적 디자인들은 상어 비늘에서 영감을 받았다.

integral   필수적인, 완전한

* Ethical considerations can be an <u>integral</u> element of biotechnology regulation.
윤리적인 배려는 생명공학 규제를 위한 필수적인 요소가 될 수 있다.

intensify   (정도·강도가) 심해지다[격렬해지다], 강화하다

* The increased power of the trade unions during and after the war not only
<u>intensified</u> industrial strife but also meant that wage cuts were slower than
price cuts.
전쟁 전후로 증가한 무역조합의 힘은 개인의 갈등을 강화했을 뿐만 아니라, 감봉이 가격인하보다 더 천천히
이루어지게 했다.

interaction   상호작용

* But he also believed that creativity is rarely a solitary process but something
brought out by social <u>interactions</u>.
그러나 그는 또한 창의성이 유일한 과정이 아니며 사회적인 상호작용에 의해 일어나는 어떤 것이라고 믿었다.

2017 제1회 서울특별시 9급

intelligible 이해할 수 있는

- Plato's allegory is a powerful metaphor for contemplating a divide between ignorance and enlightenment — between the "visible"world and the "intelligible" realm.

  플라톤의 풍자는 무지함과 깨달음 사이의 구분-"보이는"세상과 "이해할 수 있는"영역 사이의 구분-을 생각하게 하는 강력한 유추이다.

2012 상반기 지방직 9급

intimacy 친밀함, 친밀감을 나타내는 말, 성행위

- Physical intimacy stops, communication stops, and you are living like roommates.

  신체적인 친밀감이 단절되고, 의사소통이 단절되고 너의 가족은 마치 룸메이트와 같이 살고 있다.

2018 제1회 지방직 9급

intimidating 위협하는

- The student who finds the state-of-the-art approach intimidating learns less than he or she might have learned by the old methods.

  최신식 접근법이 위협적이라고 생각하는 학생들은 그들이 구식 방법으로 배운 것보다 덜 배우게 된다.

2017 지방직 9급, 2012 상반기 지방직 9급, 2009 행정안전부 9급

intuition 직관력, 직감

- I just have confidence in my intuition.

  나는 단지 내 직관에 자신을 갖는다.

- conclusions that contradict initial intuition

  초기의 직관과는 모순되는 결론

2008 상반기 지방직 9급

invariably 변함[예외]없이, 언제나

- When I ordered tea and toast in a restaurant, invariably I received tea and a cheese sandwich.

  내가 레스토랑에서 차와 토스트를 주문할 때면, 나는 언제나 차와 치즈 샌드위치를 받는다.

irrelevant   관련이 없는, 무관한, 상관없는

- Your sympathy is <u>irrelevant</u> to the morality of your action.
  당신의 동정심은 당신의 행동의 도덕성과는 관련이 없다.

leftover   (식사 후에) 남은 음식, (과거의) 잔재[유물]

- Foxes often trail the mighty bears, hoping for <u>leftovers</u> from a kill.
  여우는 흔히 살육으로부터 남은 음식을 기대하며 거대한 곰들을 뒤쫓는다.
- The islanders exchanged their oil—burning furnaces for centralized plants that burned <u>leftover</u> straw or wood chips to produce heat and hot water.
  섬사람들은 열과 온수를 생산하기 위해서 석유를 태우는 그들의 용광로를 쓰다 남은 짚과 나뭇조각을 태우는 중앙 집중식 발전소로 바꾸었다.

lord   주(보통 the lord), 장, 지배자, 주인, [영국] 귀족

- Due to the widespread use in sports of anabolic steroids, the <u>lords</u> of the game must accept that the very integrity of the game is at stake.
  스포츠에서 근육강화제의 광범위한 복용문제 때문에그 게임의 주인인 선수들은 바로 그러한진정성이 위험에 처해 있다는 사실을 받아들여야 한다.

likelihood   가능성, (어떤 일이 있을) 공산

- Did the <u>likelihood</u> of being hired depend on qualifications?
  취업이 될 가능성은 자격증에 달려있을까?

lucrative   유리한, 이익이 있는, 수지맞는, 돈벌이가 되는 (=profitable, money—making, profit—making)

- The oldest brother now has a very <u>lucrative</u> position.
  큰형은 현재 아주 돈벌이가 되는 자리에 있다.
- Hindustan Lever has built a <u>lucrative</u> business in Africa and India selling brand—name consumer goods, from lotion to salt.
  힌두스탄 레버는 아프리카와 인도에 수익성이 좋은 회사를 세워 로션에서 소금에 이르기까지 유명한 소비재를 판다.

malefactor 악인

* The police spent seven months working on the crime case but were never able to determine the identity of the malefactor.
  경찰은 7개월 동안 범죄사건을 조사했지만, 결국 범인의 신원을 밝혀낼 수 없었다.

mandatory 명령의, 통치를 위임받은, 강제적인, 의무의(=obligatory) ; 수임자, 위임 통치국(=mandatary)

* Consumer advocates call for additional testing of crops and mandatory labeling of genetically engineered products.
  소비자 옹호자들은 곡물에 대해 추가적인 실험과 유전자 조작 생산물 표시를 의무화할 것을 요구한다.

* Schooling is mandatory for all children in the United States.
  미국에서 학교 교육은 모든 연령대에게 의무적이다.

manipulate 조종하다, 조작하다, 다루다

* It is related to our conscious thoughts and our ability to manipulate symbols and language.
  그 정보는 우리는 의식적인 생각과 상징과 언어를 다룰 수 있는 능력과 연관되어 있다.

material 물질, 재료, 용구, 자료, 인격적 요소 ; 물질적인, 물질의, 구체적인

* The material in the unconscious is not forgotten or dormant.
  무의식 속에서의 인격적 요소는 잊혀지거나 잠자고 있는 것이 아니다.

* So are a good reading background and a knowledge of nonprint materials and computers.
  또한 좋은 독서 배경과 비인쇄물 그리고 컴퓨터 지식이 필수적이다.

medieval   **중세(풍)의, 고풍의, 구식의**

* <u>Medieval</u> kingdoms did not become constitutional republics overnight ; on the contrary, the change was gradual.
  중세 왕국은 하룻밤 사이 갑작스레 입헌 공화국이 된 것이 아니었다. 그와 반대로 그 변화는 점진적인 것이었다.

* <u>Medieval</u> people did not distinguish between entertainment and general merriment, of the sort that anyone could take part in at festive times.
  중세 사람들은 엔터테인먼트와 축제 기간에 누구나 참가할 수 있는 그런 종류인 일반적인 떠들썩함을 구별하지 않았다.

meditate   **명상하다, 묵상하다, 꾀하다, 계획하다**

* If you have many gifts, and the power to understand, even if you <u>meditate</u> night and day how to promote the welfare of the world, it shall profit you little if you have not joy.
  여러분이 많은 재능과 이해력을 가지고 있다면, 세상의 복지를 증진할 수 있는 방법을 밤낮으로 꾀할지라도, 기쁨을 갖고 있지 않다면 여러분에게 거의 도움이 되지 않을 것이다.

* There is more than one way to <u>meditate</u>.
  명상하는 데에는 하나 이상의 방법이 있다.

meditation   **명상, 심사숙고, 고찰, 명상록**

* This type of <u>meditation</u> is designed to help you calm your breathing, relax muscles, and keep anxious thoughts away.
  이런 종류의 명상은 당신이 숨쉬기를 차분하게 하고, 근육을 이완시키고, 그리고 걱정스런 생각들을 멀리 하도록 도와준다.

misguided   **잘못 이해한**

* The notion that a product tested without branding is somehow being more objectively appraised is entirely <u>misguided</u>.
  브랜드를 가리고 테스트한 제품이 다소 더 객관적으로 평가되고 있다는 생각은 완전히 잘못된 것이다.

mitigate   경감[완화] 시키다

- Of course, there are costs to this growth as well—in terms of environment, social cohesion, and economic equality, which each government needs to monitor and mitigate—but let's stop downplaying the economic benefits, and let's stop pretending that the antiglobalization advocates have any realistic strategy for bringing many people out of poverty quickly.

  물론, 이러한 성장에는 대가가 있다- 환경적, 사회적 결속, 그리고 경제적 평등이라는 점에서, 또한 각각의 정부가 이것들의 감시와 완화를 위해 필요로 하는- 하지만 그 경제적인 이익을 경시하지 말고 세계화에 반대하는 옹호자들은 많은 사람들을 가난에서부터 빠른 시간에 벗어나게 할 수 있는 전략을 가지고 있는 체 하는 것을 멈추자.

molt   (새가)털을 갈다, (곤충 등이)허물벗다,(동물이)뿔을갈다, 털갈이, 털갈이 시기, 벗은 허물

- As the weather changes, joggers, like some exotic species of bird, begin to molt.

  날씨가 변화함에 따라, 조깅하는 사람들은 마치 몇몇 이국적인 종류의 새들과 같이 털갈이(*운동운동 갈아입는 것을 비유)를 시작한다.

muzzle   재갈을 물리다

- Man has continued to be disobedient to authorities who tried to muzzle new thoughts and to the authority of long-established opinions which declared a change to be nonsense.

  인간은 새로운 사상을 퍼뜨리지 못하게 한 정부 당국과 변화를 무의미한 것으로 선언한 오랫동안 확립된 의견의 권위에 계속해서 복종하지 않았다.

nasty   (아주 나빠서) 끔찍한, (성격·행동 등이) 못된, 위험한, 심각한, 추잡한

- The weather has been nasty for half a month.

  날씨는 보름 동안 형편 없었다.

- I knew he was a nasty piece of work.

  나는 그가 형편없는 줄 이미 알고 있었어.

necessary 필요한, 필연적인, 불가피한

- Sponsorship is <u>necessary</u> for a successful career.
  후원은 성공적인 경력을 쌓기 위해 필수적이다.

necessity 필수품, 불가결한 것, 필요(성), 필연(성)

- A new idea, inconsistent with some of the beliefs which he holds, means the <u>necessity</u> of rearranging his mind ; and this process is laborious, requiring a painful expense of brain-energy.
  그가 가지고 있는 믿음들과 모순되는 새로운 생각들은 그의 정신을 재조정할 필요성을 의미한다. 그리고 이런 과정은 힘들고 뇌 에너지의 고통스런 희생을 요구한다.

neglect 무시하다, (무관심·부주의 등으로) ~하지 않다, (의무·일 등을) 게을리하다 ; 태만, 무시

- He <u>neglected</u> to learn how to stop his skates.
  그는 스케이트를 멈추는 방법을 배우는 것을 간과했다.
- Everyone sometimes forgets or <u>neglects</u> something.
  누구나 때때로 무언가를 잊어버리거나 소홀히 한다.

neuroscience 신경과학

- For much of the history of modern <u>neuroscience</u>, the adult brain was believed to be a fixed structure that, once damaged, could not be repaired.
  현대 신경과학의 역사상 성인의 뇌는 고정된 구조여서 한번 손상이 되면 치유할 수 없다고 믿어져 왔다.

nuisance 성가신[귀찮은] 사람[것/일], 골칫거리, (법의 제지를 받을 수 있는) 소란[방해] 행위

- It is a great <u>nuisance</u> that knowledge cannot be acquired without trouble.
  지식이 문제없이 받아들여질 수 없다는 것은 커다란 골칫거리이다.

2017 인사혁신처, 2006 중앙선거관리위원회 9급

obligation　　의무, 책임, 구속, 채권 관계

* The net result in the long run is substantially the same to each person, but through this system the principles of kinship <u>obligation</u> and the morality of sharing food have been emphasized.
장기적으로 최종적인 결과는 각자의 사람에게 동등하지만 이러한 체계를 통해 친족관계의 의무원칙과 음식을 나누는데 있어 도덕성이 강조된다.

2017 지방직 9급, 2014 사회복지직, 2014 서울특별시 9급

observation　　관찰, 감시, 주목, 주의, 관찰력

* But the big problem is that there is the variable of human <u>observation</u>.
그러나 큰 문제는 인간의 관찰이라는 변수가 있다는 것이다.

2017 지방직 9급 추가선발

occur　　발생하다, 일어나다

* However, should understanding not <u>occur</u>, you will find yourself soon becoming drowsy.
그러나 이해를 하지 못한다면(이해가 발생하지 않는다면) 곧 졸고 있는 당신을 발견하게 될 것이다.

* In North Korea, only Hangul is used, while in South Korea, Chinese characters still <u>occur</u> in particular contexts.
북한에서는 오직 한글만 사용되는 반면에 대한민국에서는 여전히 특정한 상황에서 한자가 발견된다.

2017 제2회 서울특별시 9급

officious　　거들먹거리는, 위세를 부리는

* But an <u>officious</u> person nowadays means a busy uninvited meddler in matters which do not belong to him/her.
그러나 위세를 부리는 사람은 지금은 그/그녀와 관련되지 않은 사건에 초청되지 않은 간섭하는 사람을 의미한다.

2010 행정안전부 9급

onward　　　앞으로[계속 이어서] 나아가는

* Timothy Osborn and Keith Briffa of UEA analysed instrument measurements of temperatures from 1856 <u>onwards</u> to establish the geographic extent of recent warming

UEA의 티모시 오스본과케이드 브리파는 1856년 이후부터 최근 온난화의 지리학적 범위를 확립하기 위해 온도 측정 기구를 분석했다.

2019 지방직 9급, 2018 제1회 서울특별시 9급

ordinary　　　보통의, 일상적인

* make yourself receptive to the moods of those whom you meet in the course of an <u>ordinary</u> day.

일상 중에 당신이 만나는 사람들의 기분을 받아들이도록 해라.

* But, just as momentously, the idea of germs gave <u>ordinary</u> people the power to influence their own lives.

그러나 똑같이 중요하게 병원균이라는 개념은 일반 사람들에게 자신들의 삶에 영향을 주는 힘을 주었다.

2016 지방직 9급, 2011 상반기 지방직 9급

outnumber　　　~보다 수가 더 많다, 수적으로 우세하다

* Just last week a new study showed that in science tests, teenage boys who scored in the top 5% <u>outnumbered</u> girls 7 to 1, while girls outperformed boys in reading comprehension.

바로 지난 주의 새로운 연구는 과학시험에서 상위 5%의 점수를 기록한 10대 소년들이 소녀들보다 7:1 로 우세했던 반면에 소녀들은 독해시험에서 소년들을 능가했다는 것을 보여주었다.

2010 행정안전부 9급

outspoken　　　(남의 기분에 신경 쓰지 않고) 노골적으로[거침없이] 말하는

* Sarah frequently hurts others when she criticizes their work because she is so <u>outspoken</u>.

사라는 그녀의 거침없는 언변으로 그들의 일을 비판하며 자주 상처를 준다.

outstanding　　　뛰어난

* An award ceremony for <u>outstanding</u> services to the publishing industry is put on hold.
  출판 산업에 대한 뛰어난 서비스에 관한 시상식은 보류되어진다.

overlook　　　간과하다, 못보다

* They <u>overlook</u> complications and exceptions, or mold them to fit into their world view.
  그들은 복합한 문제들과 예외들을 간과하거나, 그것들을 틀에 넣어 그들의 세계관에 맞춘다.

overwhelming　　　압도적인, 불가항력의, 굉장한, 극도의

* Therapists examining the Friends Reunited Phenomenon say that the pull of an old relationship, particularly a first love, can be <u>overwhelming</u>, particularly to those who feel unhappy, unloved, neglected, irritated or just suffused with boredom in their middle-aged marriages.
  친구 재회 현상을 연구하는 치료 전문가에 의하면 불행하거나 사랑 받지 못하거나 무시당하거나 짜증을 느끼거나 단지 중년의 결혼 생활의 지겨움으로 가득 차 있는 사람에게 과거의 관계, 특히 첫사랑에 대한 매력이 압도적일 수 있다고 한다.
* Because of the <u>overwhelming</u> number of entries last year, we're making one contest change this year.
  작년 출품작들의 압도적인 수로 인하여 이번 해에 우리는 한 가지 경연대회의 변화를 만들 것입니다.

palatable　　　맛있는, 마음에 드는, 구미에 맞는

* It would be fine if we could swallow the powder of profitable information made <u>palatable</u> by the jam of fiction.
  우리가 허구의 잼에 의해 맛있게 만들어진 유익한 정보의 가루를 먹을 수 있다면 좋을 것이다.
* Our main dish did not have much flavor, but I made it more <u>palatable</u> by adding condiments.
  메인 요리가 맛이 별로 없었지만, 나는 조미료를 첨가하여 요리를 좀 더 맛있게 만들었다.

paramount　　　다른 무엇보다 중요한

- The paramount duty of the physician is to do no harm.
  의사의 가장 중요한 의무는 해를 끼치지 않는 것이다.

pathway　　　(사람만이 다닐 수 있는) 좁은 길, 오솔길, (생화학) 경로

- For a start, understanding the neurochemical pathways that regulate social attachments may help to deal with defects in people's ability to form relationships.
  그 시작으로, 사회적 애착을 조절하는 신경 화학 물질 통로에 대해 이해하는 것이 어쩌면 관계를 형성하려는 인간 능력의 결함을 다루는 데 도움이 될 수 있다.

peer　　　(나이 · 신분이 같거나 비슷한) 또래[동배]

- Others do not want their children to have to worry about "peer pressure", or social pressure from friends.
  다른 사람들은 그들의 자녀가 "또래 집단이 주는 압박감" 또는 친구들로부터 받는 사회적 압력에 대해 걱정해야 하는 것을 원치 않는다.
- Many have friendships with members of the opposite sex, good relationships with their parents and families; most are popular with their peers.
  많은 사람들이 이성 친구와 교제하며, 부모님과 가족들과도 좋은 관계를 가지고 있다.

penalize　　　(법 · 규칙을 어긴 데 대해) 처벌하다, (부당한 처사로 사람을)불리하게 만들다

- Conserving water is typically a good thing—except when you're penalized for your frugality.
  물 절약은 당신이 물을 절약한 것으로 처벌을 받지만 않는다면 전형적으로 좋은 일이다.

penetrate　　　관통하다

- Lewis Alfred Ellison, died in 1916 after an operation to cure internal wounds suffering after shards from a 100-lb ice block penetrated his abdomen when it was dropped while being loaded into a hopper.
  Lewis Alfred Ellison은 1916년 100파운드짜리 얼음 덩어리가 호퍼로 운반되는 도중 그것이 떨어져 그 얼음의 날카로운 부분이 그의 복부를 관통하여 고통 받다가 내부 상처를 치료하기 위한 수술을 받은 후 사망하였다.

performance   실행, 성과, 성적, 행동, 상연, 연기

* It is common knowledge that ability to do a particular job and <u>performance</u> on the job do not always go hand in hand.
  어떤 특정한 일을 하는 능력과 업무 수행은 항상 병행되는 것이 아니라는 것은 상식이다.

* Its consequences such as sleepiness and impaired psychomotor <u>performance</u> are similar to those of sleep deprivation.
  졸음이나 손상된 정신운동수행과 같은 이것의 영향은 수면 부족의 영향과 같다.

persuade   ~을 설득시키다, 믿게 하다, 확인시키다, 납득시키다

* He is impossible for us to <u>persuade</u>.
  우리가 그를 설득하는 건 불가능하다.

* It is another to <u>persuade</u> people to respect it.
  사람들에게 그것을 존중하도록 설득하는 것이다.

pervasive   만연하는

* In those countries, the widespread availability of safe and reliable contraception combined with the <u>pervasive</u> postponement of childbearing as well as with legal access to abortion in most of them has resulted in a sharp reduction of unwanted births and, consequently, in a reduction of the number of adoptable children.
  그러한 나라들에서는 광범위한 안전하고 믿을 만한 피임의 이용 가능성이, 만연하는 출산의 연기뿐만 아니라 낙태에 대한 법적 허용까지 결합되어, 그 결과, 대부분은 원치 않는 출산의 빠른 감소가 이뤄졌다.

petition   탄원(서), 청원(서), 신청(서)

* In the weeks following the referendum, millions of people signed a <u>petition</u> asking for a second referendum.
  총선 몇 주후 많은 사람들이 재선을 요구하는 진정서를 냈다.

phenomenon　　　현상, 사상, 사건(pl. phenomena)

* As this is a recent <u>phenomenon</u>, we have yet to see what happens when one split-named person marries another split-named person.

  이런 일이 최근의 현상이다 보니 우리는 하나로 된 두 성을 가진 사람이 그와 같은 또 다른 사람과 결혼을 하게 되는 때에는 어떤 일이 일어날지 두고 봐야 한다.

* Novelty-induced time expansion is a well-characterized <u>phenomenon</u> which can be investigated under laboratory conditions.

  새로움으로 유도된 시간 확장은 실험실 조건 아래에서 조사될 수 있는 잘 특징지어진 현상이다.

physiological　　　생리적인

* At the two week point without exercising, there are a multitude of <u>physiological</u> markers that naturally reveal a reduction of fitness level.

  운동을 하지 않고 2주가 되면 운동 강도가 감소되었을 때 자연스럽게 나타나는 신체적인 지표들이 많아진다.

pictorial　　　그림을 이용한, 그림이 포함된, 그림[회화]의

* Signs are simply <u>pictorial</u> representations of external reality

  단순히 그림을 이용하여 외적 현실에 대해 묘사한 기호들

* Countries have taken more restrictive measures, including taxation, <u>pictorial</u> health warnings and prohibitions on advertising and promotion, against cigarette products over the past four decades.

  여러 국가들은 지난 40년 동안 담배 제품에 대해 조세, 그림으로 된 건강 경고문구, 그리고 광고와 홍보 금지 등을 포함한 더욱 제한적인 조치를 취해 왔다.

pivotal　　　중추적인, 중요한

* Some athletes indicated that negative weight - related comments from family were <u>pivotal</u> events in the development of eating disorders.

  몇몇 운동선수들은 가족으로부터의 체중과 관련된 부정적인 언급이 식이장애의 발달에 있어 중요한 사건이라는 것을 보여주었다.

plasticity 　　가소성

* If the area of the brain associated with speech is destroyed, the brain may use <u>plasticity</u> to cause other areas of the brain not originally associated with this speech to learn the skill as a way to make up for lost cells.
  만약 언어와 관련된 뇌의 부분이 파괴된다면, 뇌는 손상된 세포를 대체하는 방법으로 언어와 원래 관련되지 않은 뇌의 다른 부분이 그 능력을 배우도록 유도하는 유연성을 사용한다.

plummet 　　급락하다

* Suddenly, someone who was so in charge may become withdrawn and sullen, and their self-esteem may <u>plummet</u>.
  갑자기 책임자가 물러나거나 침울해지고 그들의 자부심은 급락할 수 있다.

pose 　　(위협·문제 등을) 제기하다

* Whether or not they dream is another question, which can be answered only by <u>posing</u> another one.
  그들이 꿈을 꾸느냐 마느냐는 다음 질문을 제기함에 의해서만 대답할 수 있는 또 다른 문제이다.

posterity 　　후세, 후대

* individuals of all nations are melted into a new race of men, whose labors and <u>posterity</u> will one day cause great changes in the world.
  모든 나라의 각 개인들은 새로운 인종으로 변형되었고, 이 인종의 후세들이 언젠가는 세계에서 거대한 변화를 가져올 것이다.

pompous 　　젠체하는, 거만한

* Don'nt be <u>pompous</u>.
  잘난 척하지 마십시오.

potential   잠재(능)력, 가능성 ; 잠재적인, 발전 가능성이 있는, 잠재력이 있는, 가능한

* Even our most receptive colleagues who embrace every new piece of new technology have a hard time keeping up with the potential.

  심지어 새로운 모든 기술 공학을 잘 따라가고 있는, 이해력 빠른 대부분의 동료들조차도 인터넷이 가진 잠재성을 따라가는 데 어려움을 느낀다.

* It shows how the new dynamics of turbo-charged globalization has the potential and power to destabilize our societies.

  그것은 터보엔진이 달린 세계화의 새로운 원동력이 얼마나 우리 사회를 불안정하게 만들 수 있는 잠재력과 힘을 가지는지를 보여준다.

* Layered upon time are a slew of other ingredients, life focus, precision, discipline, and desire.

  삶의 초점, 정확성, 그리고 욕구 등의 많은 다른 구성요소가 시간을 두고 겹겹이 쌓이는 것이다.

precedence   우선(함)

* In other cultures, the group clearly takes precedence.

  다른 문화에서는 명백하게 집단이 우선권을 얻는다.

precipitation   강수량

* It's also shifting precipitation patterns and setting animals on the move.

  그것은 또한 강수 패턴을 바꾸고 동물들의 이동을 일으킨다.

precisely   정밀하게

* The amount of information gathered by the eyes as contrasted with the ears has not been precisely calculated.

  귀와 대조하여 눈에 의해 수집되는 정보의 양은 정확하게 계산되지 않아왔다.

2015 제1회 지방직 9급, 2010 행정안전부 9급

precision   정확(성), 정밀(성), 신중함

* However, this <u>precision</u> cannot be achieved without real appreciation of the subtleties of language.
  그러나 이 정확성은 언어의 중요한 세부 요소들의 진정한 공감 없이는 성취될 수 없다.

2015 인사혁신처 9급, 2014 안전행정부 9급

predict   예언하다, 예측하다, 예보하다(=foretell)

* She <u>predicted</u> that I would enter the university that I wanted to go to.
  그녀는 내가 가고 싶어 하는 대학에 입학할 것이라고 예언했다.
* The number of cellular phone subscribers in Asia is <u>predicted</u> to rise from the current figure of around 10 million to 72 million by the year 2,000.
  아시아에서 휴대폰 가입자 수는 현재 대략 1,000만 명에서 2,000년까지 7,200만 명으로 늘어날 것으로 전망된다.
* Yeah, think ahead of the speaker and try to <u>predict</u> what's coming next.
  예, 연설자보다 먼저 생각해 보고 다음에 무엇이 올지 예측해 보도록 노력하라.

2019 국가직 9급

prejudice   편견

* With his ability to fuse serious content with humorous style, Hughes attacked racial <u>prejudice</u> in a way that was natural and witty.
  엄숙한 문제를 해학적인 스타일과 결합시키는 능력으로, Hughes는 자연스럽고 재치있는 방식으로 인종편견을 공격했다.

2017 인사혁신처

premise   전제

* Psychodrama as a form of group therapy started with <u>premises</u> that were quite alien to the Freudian worldview that mental illness essentially occurs within the psyche or mind.
  집단치료의 한 형태로서의 심리극은 정신질환이 본질적으로 정신 또는 마음에서 일어난다는 프로이드의 견해와는 다른 전제에서 출발했다.

preponderance (수적으로) 우세함[더 많음]

* According to government figures, the preponderance of jobs in the next century will be in service-related fields, such as health and business.
정부 발표 자료에 따르면, 다음 세기의 일자리의 수적 우세는 의료나 비즈니스와 같은 서비스 관련 분야에서 이루어 질 것이라고 한다.

presidency 대통령직[임기], 회장직[임기]

* Even the dreamer himself, Dr. Martin Luther King, Jr., might not have imagined that 40 short years after his murder, we would be planning an inauguration of the first man of African descent to ascend to the presidency.
심지어 몽상가인 마틴 루터 킹 주니어 그 자신조차 그가 살해 된지 겨우 40년 만에 아프리카 혈통의 첫 번째 사람이 대통령직에 오르는 대통령 취임식을 우리가 준비하고 있을 것이라고는 상상하지 않았을 것이다.

prerequisite (무엇이 있기 위해서는 꼭 필요한) 전제 조건

* But limited income is hardly a prerequisite for developing this kind of empathy and social responsiveness.
그러나 제한된 수입원이 이러한 종류의 공감대와 사회적 민감성을 발달시키는 전제 조건은 아니다.

* As a prerequisite for fertilization, pollination is essential to the production of fruit and seed crops and plays an important part in programs designed to improve plants by breeding.
수정을 위한 전제 조건으로, 수분은 과일과 종자식물의 생산에 필수적이며, 번식을 통해 식물을 개량하기 위해 고안된 프로그램에서 중요한 역할을 한다.

pretend ~인 체하다, 가장하다, 사칭하다, (특히 거짓으로) 주장하다

* I could tell he was only pretending to read, because his book was upside down.
그의 책이 거꾸로 뒤집어져 있었기 때문에 나는 그가 단지 책을 읽는 척했다는 것을 알 수 있었다.

* You get up in the morning with a bad headache or an attack of depression, yet you face the day and cope with other people, pretending that nothing is wrong.
당신이 아침에 일어나서 극심한 두통이 있고 우울감이 몰려와도 당신은 아무렇지도 않은 체 하며 다른 사람들을 만나고 하루를 보내야 한다.

2018 인사혁신처

primary   주요한

* It can be caused by another disorder, or it can be a <u>primary</u> disorder.
  그것은 다른 질환에 의해 생길 수도 있거나 이것이 주요한 질병일 수도 있다.

2017 제1회 서울특별시 9급

primordial   원시적인

* It was cosmic microwave background radiation, a residue of the <u>primordial</u> explosion of energy and matter that suddenly gave rise to the universe some 13.8 billion years ago.
  그것은 우주 마이크로파 배경복사였고, 이는 138억 년 전 우주를 생겨나게 했던 에너지와 물체들의 원시 폭발의 잔여물들이었다.

2009 상반기 지방직 9급

procuring   (특히 어렵게) 구하다[입수하다], 매춘부를 알선하다

* We can rid ourselves of our suspiciousness only by <u>procuring</u> more knowledge.
  우리는 더 많은 지식을 얻음으로써 의심을 없앨 수 있다.

2016 서울특별시 9급

prodigal   (돈 · 시간 · 에너지 · 물자를) 낭비하는

* He was born to a wealthy family in New York in 1800's. This circumstance allowed him to lead a <u>prodigal</u> existence for much of his life.
  그는 1800년대 뉴욕의 부유한 가정에서 태어났다. 이런 환경은 그에게 그의 삶의 대부분을 호화로운 상황에서 지내게 만들었다.

2006 서울시 9급, 2005 대구시 9급

productive   생산적인, 다산의, 풍부한, 영리적인

* Here are some tips to make your search more <u>productive</u>.
  여기에 당신의 구직을 좀 더 효율적으로 하는 몇 가지의 조언이 있다.

* For instance, about half of the top soil of Iowa, the state whose agriculture <u>productivity</u> is among the highest in the U.S., has been eroded in the last 150 years.
  예를 들면, 미국에서 가장 높은 농업 생산력을 지난 Iowa주의 상층부 토양의 반 정도가 지난 150년 동안 침식되어 왔다.

2015 사회복지직 9급, 2011 법원행정처 9급, 2005 중앙인사위원회 9급

profound	깊은, 심원한, 뜻 깊은, 난해한

* The Pacific is the deepest ocean, with a bottom area at more <u>profound</u> depths than any other ocean.
  태평양은 다른 어떤 바다보다도 더 깊은 곳에 해저를 가지고 있는 가장 깊은 바다이다.

* Asian art and music have had <u>profound</u> influences on the West across the centuries.
  수 세기에 걸쳐 아시아의 예술과 음악은 서구에 엄청난 영향을 미쳤다.

2016 인사혁신처 9급

profuse	풍부한, 많은, 다량의

* Disney's work draws heavily from fairy tales, myths, and folklore, which are <u>profuse</u> in archetypal elements.
  디즈니의 작품은 동화, 신화 그리고 민속 문화에서 많은 것을 차용하는데 여기에는 전형적인 요소들이 풍부하다.

2017 인사혁신처, 2013 안전행정부 · 서울특별시 9급

promote	증진하다, 촉진하다, 장려하다, 승진시키다

* Plato grasped which sorts of experiences helped <u>promote</u> the development of truly human individuals.
  플라톤은 어떤 종류의 경험들이 진실로 인간적인 개인들의 발전을 촉진하는 데 도움이 되는지를 파악하고 있었다.

* He relied heavily on theatrical techniques, including role-playing and improvisation, as a means to <u>promote</u> creativity and general social trust.
  그는 창의성과 사회적 신뢰를 증가시키기 위한 수단으로 역할극과 즉흥극을 포함한 연극적인 기법을 상당히 의존했다.

2007 행정자치부 9급

prop	지주, 버팀목, 받침대, (연극 · 영화에 쓰이는) 소품

* You lose all of the <u>props</u> that generally support you, and all of the familiar cues that provide information about what to do.
  너는 일반적으로 너를 지지해주던 버팀목과 무엇을 해야 할지에 대한 안내를 제공하는 모든 친숙한 신호를 잃어버린다.

propel

(몰거나 밀거나 해서) 나아가게 하다, (사람을 특정한 방향·상황으로) 몰고 가다

* It can <u>propel</u> you to do better work or to complete work on time.
  그것은 당신이 일을 더 잘하게 하거나 또는 제시간에 일을 끝마칠 수 있도록 몰 수 있다.

* Obviously, the higher you raise your per-hour worth while upholding your priorities, the more you can <u>propel</u> your efforts toward meeting your goals, because you have more resources at your disposal — you have either more money or more time, whichever you need most.
  왜냐하면 당신은 당신이 원하는 대로 쓸 수 있는 자원을 더 많이 가지고 있기 때문이다. – 당신이 가장 필요로 하는 것이 무엇이든, 당신은 더 많은 돈과 더 많은 시간을 가지고 있기 때문이다.

property

재산, 소유물, 상품, 부동산

* The salesman tried to convince a group of investors that the <u>properties</u> he was selling would soon be worth much more money than he was asking.
  그 외판원은 그가 팔고 있는 상품들이 곧 그가 요구하는 가격보다 더 많은 자산 가치가 있게 될 것이라고 많은 투자자들에게 확신시키려고 노력하였다.

* He grew up, had a family, and bought <u>property</u> in Stratford, but he worked in London, the center of English theater.
  그가 성장해서 가족을 가졌고, 스트래퍼드에서 부동산을 구매했지만 그는 영국 극장의 중심인 런던에서 일했다.

* In Locke's defense of private <u>property</u>, the significant point is what happens when we mix our labor with God's land.
  사유재산에 대한 로크의 방어에 따르면 중요한 요점은 우리가 신이 내려준 토지에 우리의 노동이 결합할 때 무엇인가가 발생하느냐이다.

proliferate

급증하다

* Children's book awards have <u>proliferated</u> in recent years.
  최근에 아동문학상이 급증하고 있다.

prolific

다작하는, 다산하는

* Crystal, one of the most <u>prolific</u> writers on English, has helped popularize that truth.
  영국에서 가장 작품을 많이 쓰는 작가 중 하나인 Crystal은 이런 사실을 대중화하는 데 기여해 왔다.

prospective   장래의, 유명한

* There are not enough adoptable children in developed countries for the residents of those countries wishing to adopt, and <u>prospective</u> adoptive parents have increasingly resorted to adopting children abroad.
  선진국에서는 아이를 입양하기 바라는 사람들을 위한 충분한 입양아가 없게 되었고, 아이를 입양하기 바라는 양부모들은 점점 더 해외에서 아이를 입양하는 것에 의존해 왔다.

prosperity   번영, 번창

* Orkney owed its <u>prosperity</u> largely to its geographical advantage and natural resources.
  Orkney는 그 지리학적인 이점과 자연 자원 덕분에 번영했다..

proverb   속담

* Actually this <u>proverb</u> is, for the most part, not true.
  하지만 대부분의 경우 이 속담은 진실이 아니다.

pupil   (특히 어린) 학생, (전문가에게서 배우는) 문하생[제자], 눈동자, 동공

* If John Wilkins, who is big and strong, doesn't go out for the football team, some <u>pupils</u> say, "Wilkins has no courage."
  만약 크고 건강한 존 윌킨스가 그 축구팀을 위해 나가지 않는다면 몇몇 학생들은 "윌킨슨은 용기가 없어"라고 말할 것이다.

pursue   추구하다

* Many African-American students have <u>pursued</u> their academic disciplines.
  많은 아프리카계 미국인 학생들이 그들의 학문분야들을 추구해오고 있다.

2016 서울특별시 9급

rebellious   (규칙 · 일반 통념 등에 대해) 반항적인

* Parents must not give up on kids who act <u>rebellious</u> or seem socially awkward.
부모들은 사회적으로 다루기 곤란해 보이거나 반항적으로 행동하는 아이들을 단념해서는 안 된다.

2013 안전행정부, 2011 행정안전부 9급

recipient   (어떤 것을) 받는 사람, 수령[수취]인

* The person whose attitude towards others is genuinely of this kind will be a source of happiness and a <u>recipient</u> of reciprocal kindness.
다른 사람들을 대하는 태도가 진정으로 이러한 사람들은 행복의 원천이 될 것이며 상호간 친절의 수혜자가 될 것이다.

2018 서울특별시 9급, 2011 행정안전부 9급

reciprocal   상호간의

* The person whose attitude towards others is genuinely of this kind will be a source of happiness and a recipient of <u>reciprocal</u> kindness.
다른 사람들을 대하는 태도가 진정으로 이러한 사람들은 행복의 원천이 될 것이며 상호간 친절의 수혜자가 될 것이다.

2017 제1회 지방직 9급

reckless   무모한

* The fear of getting hurt didn't prevent him from engaging in <u>reckless</u> behaviors.
다치는 것에 대한 두려움도 그가 무모한 행동을 하는 것을 막지 못했다.

2011 행정안전부 9급

reclaim   (분실하거나 빼앗긴 물건 등을) 되찾다, (황무지 등을) 개간하다, (폐품을) 재활용하다, (중독자 · 범죄자 등을) 갱생시키다

* The viability of <u>reclaimed</u> water for indirect potable reuse should be assessed with regard to quantity and reliability of raw water supplies, the quality of reclaimed water, and cost effectiveness.
2차적인 식수로서 재활용 재생수를 사용할 수 있는가의 문제는 상수의 양과 신뢰도, 재생수의 질, 그리고 비용 효율성에 관련하여 평가되어야 한다.

recognize   인식, 인정하다

* leadership theories gradually <u>recognized</u> the active and important role that followers play in the leadership process.
리더십 이론들은 점차 따르는 사람들이 리더십 과정에서 수행하는 적극적이고 중요한 역할을 인식했다.

reconcile   (두 가지 이상의 생각 · 요구 등을) 조화시키다, 화해시키다, (어쩔 수 없는 불쾌한 상황을 체념하고) 받아들이다

* No surprise then that its society can <u>reconcile</u> another set of opposing forces
그것의 사회가 또 다른 반대세력들과 화해할 수 있다는 것은 놀라운 것이 아니다.

recurrent   되풀이되는, 재발되는

* In 2003, Amos Tversky, my younger colleague, and I met over lunch and shared our <u>recurrent</u> errors of judgment.
2003년, 나보다 젊은 동료였던 Amos Tversky와 나는 점심식사를 하며 되풀이되는 판단의 오류에 대해 공유하기 위해 만났다.

redeem   회복하다, 되찾다

* He dismally fails the first two, but <u>redeems</u> himself in the concluding whale episode.
그는 우울하게 처음 두 번은 실패했지만 마지막에서 만회하였다.

* The goldsmiths accepted the gold for storage, giving the owner a receipt stating that the gold could be <u>redeemed</u> at a later date.
금세공인들은 보관을 위한 금을 받아들였고, 그 소유주에게 영수증을 주어서 나중에 그 금을 되찾을 수 있도록 했다.

reflective   반사하는

* Whether a guffaw at a joke or a <u>reflective</u> chuckle greeting a sarcastic remark, laughter is the audience's means of ratifying the performance.
농담에 대한 시끄러운 웃음이거나 비꼬는 발언에 반응하는 반사적인 싱그레 웃음이든지 간에 웃음은 공연을 받아들이는 청중의 수단이다.

relative   친척, 친지

* The young woman wears a full-length white or pastel-colored dress and is attended by fourteen friends and <u>relatives</u> who serve as maids of honor and male escorts.
  젊은 여성은 흰색이나 파스텔 색의 긴 드레스를 입고 남자 에스코트와 여자 들러리 역할을 하는 14명의 친구, 친지들의 시중을 받는다.

* Amy Lang, studies the scales on the shortfin mako, a <u>relative</u> of the great white shark.
  Amy Lang은 백상아리의 친척관계인 청상아리의 비늘을 연구했다.

release   방출하다

* The major threat to plants, animals, and people is the extremely toxic chemicals <u>releasing</u> into the air and water.
  식물, 동물 그리고 사람들에게 가장 큰 위협은 공기와 물로 방출된 독성 화학물이다.

reliability   신뢰할 수 있음, 신뢰도, 확실성

* The viability of reclaimed water for indirect potable reuse should be assessed with regard to quantity and <u>reliability</u> of raw water supplies, the quality of reclaimed water, and cost effectiveness.
  2차적인 식수로서 재활용 재생수를 사용할 수 있는가의 문제는 상수의 양과 신뢰도, 재생수의 질, 그리고 비용 효율성에 관련하여 평가되어야 한다.

repetitive   반복적인

* Simply asking people to estimate the length of time they are exposed to a train of stimuli shows that novel stimuli simply seem to last longer than <u>repetitive</u> or unremarkable ones.
  단순히 사람들에게 일련의 자극에 노출된 시간의 길이를 추정하도록 물어보는 것은 새로운 자극이 반복적이고 평범한 자극보다 더 오래 지속된다는 것을 보여준다.

replacement 교체, 대체

* Depending on the circumstances, the home language may succumb completely to the language of the invaders, in which case we talk about <u>replacement</u>.
  상황에 따라 모국어는 침략자들의 언어에 완전히 굴복할 수도 있는데, 그 경우 우리는 대체 언어에 대해 이야기한다.
* If anything, the role of school food service as a <u>replacement</u> for what was once a family function has been expanded.
  한때 가정의 기능이었던 것의 대체로 학교급식서비스의 역할이 확장되었다.

replicate (정확히) 모사[복제]하다, 자기 복제를 하다

* One bacterium that survives keeps <u>replicating</u> because it is not susceptible to the drug treatment.
  살아남는 하나의 박테리아는 약물요법에 민감하기 때문에 계속하여 복제한다.
* While we sometimes take these standbys for granted, the flavor of allium vegetables can not be <u>replicated</u>.
  그리고 심장병이나 암을 예방해 주는 물질을 포함하고 있는 그들의 건강적인 이점도 마찬가지로 흉내 낼 수 없다.

reptile 파충류 동물, 파행 동물(=crawling animal), 비열한 사람, 악랄한 인간 ; 파행하는, 기어 다니는, 파충류의, 비열한

* <u>Reptiles</u> and fish may no doubt be found in swarms and shoals.
  파충류와 어류는 아마 무리로 발견될 수도 있다.
* Most <u>reptiles</u> are apparently quite careless about their eggs, which are left for sun and season to hatch.
  대부분의 파충류들은 그들의 알에 대해 명백하게 매우 관심이 없었으며, 알들은 부화를 위한 태양과 시간에 버려지곤 했다.

reputation 평판, 세평, 명성, 호평

* George Stephenson gained a <u>reputation</u> for working with the primitive steam engines employed in mines in the northeast of England and in Scotland.
  조지 스티븐산은 영국 북동지역과 스코틀랜드의 탄광에 사용된 초기 증기기관과 관련된 일을 하면서 명성을 얻었다.
* The <u>reputation</u> of Genghis Khan as may be worse than the reality.
  칭기즈칸의 완전히 무자비한 전사에 대한 명성은 실제보다 더 악화되었을 수도 있다.

residue 　　　잔여[잔류]물, 잔여 유산

* Look for all natural, non-toxic products that break down without leaving harmful <u>residues</u> in the environment.
  환경에 어떠한 해로운 잔여물도 남기지 않고 분해되는 완전 천연이자 무독성의 상품을 찾아라.
* It was cosmic microwave background radiation, a <u>residue</u> of the primordial explosion of energy and matter that suddenly gave rise to the universe some 13.8 billion years ago.
  그것은 우주 마이크로파 배경복사였고, 이는 138억 년 전 우주를 생겨나게 했던 에너지와 물체들의 원시 폭발의 잔여물들이었다.

resistance 　　　저항력

* It improved <u>resistance</u> of crops to diseases and created massive job opportunities within the industrial and agricultural sectors.
  녹색혁명은 작물의 질병 저항력을 증대시켜 주었고, 산업과 농업 분야의 일자리 대방출을 가져왔다.

restrict 　　　제한하다

* Leadership is not <u>restricted</u> to the influence exerted by someone in a particular position or role.
  리더십은 특정한 위치나 역할에 있는 누군가에 의해 행사되는 영향에만 국한되지 않는다.

resurgence 　　　재기, 부활

* Perhaps the brightest spot in the contemporary landscape of American higher education is the <u>resurgence</u> of interest in engaging students in civic life beyond campus.
  미국 고등교육의 당대 현실에서 가장 괜찮은 점은 아마 학생들이 캠퍼스를 넘어서 시민생활에 몰두하도록 하는 것에 대한 관심의 부활이다.

respondents   응답자, 설문 참여자

* The latest questionnaire found that well over 60 percent of the <u>respondents</u> chose television over other media as their major source of information.

  최근 설문조사는 60퍼센트를 훨씬 넘어선 응답자들이 그들이 얻는 정보의 주요 원천으로 다른 매체 보다 텔레비전을 선택했다는 것을 발견했다.

retaliation   (같은 수단으로의) 앙갚음, 보복

* Never does he harbor resentment, store up petty grudges, or waste energy or thought by means of revenge or <u>retaliation</u>.

  그는 결코 원한을 품지 않으며, 사소한 불만을 쌓아두지 않으며, 복수나 앙갚음으로 정력이나 생각을 낭비하지 않는다.

* In <u>retaliation</u>, he dissolved Chechnyan autonomy in 1944, and ordered the deportation of the ethnic Chechnyan population to Central Asia.

  그는 복수로 1944년에 체첸 자치국을 해산시켰고, 체첸 민족을 중앙아시아로 추방했다.

retain   (계속) 유지[보유]하다, 간직[함유]하다

* An experiment done on American astronauts made it clear that physical activity is important to <u>retain</u> strong, healthy bones.

  미국 우주비행사들을 대상으로 한 실험에서 강하고 튼튼한 뼈를 유지하기 위해서는 신체활동이 매우 중요하다는 것이 입증되었다.

retreat   후퇴하다

* The paper suggests that warming temperatures have caused bumblebee populations to <u>retreat</u> from the southern limits of their travels by as much as 190 miles since the 1970s.

  그 연구지는 1970년대부터 따뜻해지고 있는 기온이 호박벌 군수를 그 이동의 남쪽 경계로부터 190마일이나 후퇴시켰음을 시사한다.

retrospect

회상, 추억, 선례의 참고, 회상에 잠기다, 소급하여 대조해 보다

* In retrospect, I was taken in by the real estate agent who had a fancy manner of talking.
  돌이켜 생각해보면, 나는 부동산 중개업자의 화려한 말솜씨에 속아 넘어간 것이다.

reveal

드러내다

* At the two week point without exercising, there are a multitude of physiological markers that naturally reveal a reduction of fitness level.
  운동을 하지 않고 2주가 되면 운동 강도가 감소되었을 때 자연스럽게 나타나는 신체적인 지표들이 많아진다.

rig

(부정한 수법으로) 조작하다, (배에 선구를) 갖추다, (장비를) 설치[장치] 하다.

* In other words, they rig the game in their favor by choosing to value things that are within their grasp.
  다시 말해서 그들은 자신이 잡을 수 있는 가치들을 선택함으로써 그들의 취향에 맞게 게임을 조작한다.

rigid

(규칙 · 방법 · 사람 등이) 엄격한, 융통성 없는, (사물 · 물질이)뻣뻣한, 단 단한, 잘 휘지 않는

* What a woman feels she has been assigned the role of silently listening audience does not mean that a man feels he has consigned her to that role—or that he necessarily likesthe rigid alignment either.
  한 여성이 자신이 조용히 듣고만 있는 청취자의 역할을 부여 받았다고 느낀다고 해서 남성이 여성에게 그러한 역할을 맡겼다고 느낀다거나 혹은 남성이 그러한 엄격한 역할배정을 반드시 좋아한다는 것을 의미하지는 않는다.

sabotage

(고의적인) 방해행위, 사보타주(*적이 사용하는 것을 막기 위해 또는 무엇 에 대한 항의의 표시로 장비, 운송 시설, 기계 등을 고의로 파괴하는 것)

* When you are passed over for a promotion or when a coworker who you think is a friend goes to lunch with the manager who is trying to sabotage your project, you probably fantasize about how great life would be if you didn't have to make money for a living.
  당신이 승진의 기회를 놓쳐 버렸거나, 친하다고 생각했던 동료가 당신의 프로젝트를 파괴하려 하는 매니저와 점심을 먹으러 갈 때, 당신은 아마 먹고 살기 위해서 돈을 벌 필요가 없었으면 얼마나 인생이 멋졌을까 하는 상상을 하게 될 것이다.

safeguard

~을 지키다, 보호하다, 호송하다 ; 보호(책), 보호 수단, 호위병, (기계 등의) 안전장치

* In those days people wanting to <u>safeguard</u> their gold had two choices.
  그 시절에 그들의 금을 보호하기를 원했던 사람들은 두 가지 선택이 있었다.

* The government is setting stringent standards on thermal pollution, since it has found present regulation to be deficient in many respects and unable to <u>safeguard</u> our waters.
  정부는 열오염에 대한 엄격한 기준을 정하고 있다. 왜냐하면 현재의 법규가 많은 점에서 불충분하고 우리의 수자원을 보호할 수 없다는 것이 밝혀졌기 때문이다.

Example The industry has a duty to _____ consumers.

▣ safeguard

---

sanctuary

보호 구역

* Humpback Whale Marine <u>Sanctuary</u> said they've been getting reports that the whales have been difficult to spot so far.
  혹등고래 해양보호 구역 전문가들은 지금까지 고래를 발견하기 어려웠다는 보고를 받고 있다고 한다.

---

scarce

부족한, 드문, 겨우, 거의 ~ 않다

* The most elusive element of all, however, appears to be francium, which is so <u>scarce</u> that it is thought that our entire planet may contain, at any given moment, fewer than twenty francium atoms.
  그러나 모든 원소 가운데 가장 파악이 어려운 것은 프랑슘인데 어떠한 때에 측정해 보아도 지구 전체에 20개 미만의 프랑슘 원소가 있다고 생각될 정도로 극히 적다.

---

schizophrenia

정신 분열증

* Defects can be disabling, and become apparent as disorders such as autism and <u>schizophrenia</u>.
  결함들은 불능화 될 수 있고 자폐증이나 정신 분열증과 같은 명백한 장애가 될 수도 있다.

scope

(무엇을 하거나 이룰 수 있는) 기회[여지/능력], (주제·조직·활동 등이 다루는) 범위, (공간의) 넓이, 길이

- The kind of interest in persons that makes for happiness is the kind that likes to observe people and finds pleasure in their individual traits that wishes to afford <u>scope</u> for the interests and pleasures of those with whom it is brought into contact without desiring to acquire power over them or to secure their enthusiastic admiration.

  행복을 향해 나아가는 사람들의 관심은 사람들을 관찰하기 좋아하고 그들의 개인적 특성들에서 기쁨을 발견하는 것이고, 사람들을 지배하는 권력을 얻거나 그들의 열광적인 칭찬을 얻기를 바라는 것 없이 이해 관계를 맺은 사람들의 관심과 즐거움에 대한 기회를 가질 수 있기를 바라는 것이다.

scrutiny

정밀 조사, 철저한 검토

- Suddenly, she was the focus of intense <u>scrutiny</u>.

  갑자기, 그녀는 진지하고 철저한 검토의 초점이 되었다.

- The outrage among Chinese residents and the global media <u>scrutiny</u> impelled the government to address the country's air pollution problem.

  중국 거주민들의 분노와 세계 미디어의 철저한 검토로 중국 정부는 국가의 공기오염 문제를 다루어야만 했다.

secure

안심하는, 안전한, 확실한, 튼튼한

- The kind of interest in persons that makes for happiness is the kind that likes to observe people and finds pleasure in their individual traits that wishes to afford scope for the interests and pleasures of those with whom it is brought into contact without desiring to acquire power over them or to <u>secure</u> their enthusiastic admiration.

  행복을 향해 나아가는 사람들의 관심은 사람들을 관찰하기를 좋아하고 그들의 개인적 특성들에서 기쁨을 발견하는 것이고, 사람들을 지배하는 권력을 얻거나 그들의 열광적인 칭찬을 확고히 하길 바라는 것 없이 이해 관계를 맺은 사람들의 관심과 즐거움에 대한 기회를 가질 수 있기를 바라는 것이다.

seductive

(성적으로) 유혹[매혹/고혹]적인, 마음을 끄는

- The well−born young Athenians who gathered around Socrates found it quite paradoxical that their hero was so intelligent, so brave, so honorable, so <u>seductive</u>−and so ugly.

  소크라테스 주위에 모인 명문가 출신의 젊은 아테네인 들은 자신들의 영웅(소크라테스)이 총명하고 용감하고 고결하지만 못생겼다는 점에서 그것이 꽤 역설적이라는 것을 발견하였다.

self-examination 　　자기반성, (질병의 징후를 발견하기 위한) 자기진단

* According to educator-counselor Joanne Bernstein, stories that confront life's problems with candor and credibility may provide insights, promote self-examination, and lead to changes in attitude and behavior.

  교육자이다 상담가인 조앤 번스테인에 의하면 솔직하고 신빙성 있게 삶의 문제들에 직면하는 이야기들은 통찰력을 제공할 수 있고 자기 성찰을 촉진하며 태도와 행동에 있어서의 변화를 가져 올 수도 있다고 한다.

sensible 　　분별 있는, 지각 있는, 상식적인, 똑똑한, 사리에 맞는

* The other saying, "love is blind" is far more sensible.

  '사랑은 맹목적이다.'라는 다른 속담이 더 사리에 맞는다.

serve 　　~에 봉사하다, ~을 섬기다, ~을 위하여 일하다, ~에 쓸모가 있다

* He based his personal philosophy on a "reverence for life" and on a deep commitment to serve humanity through thought and action.

  그는 그의 개인 철학의 바탕을 '생명에 대한 존경심' 그리고 생각과 행동을 통해 인류에 봉사하는 깊은 헌신에 두었다.

* The worldwide fiber optic network is constantly expanding and is never likely to be really completed as points are added to better serve customers.

  범세계적 섬유 광학 네트워크는 계속해서 확장되고 있고 소비자들에게 더 나은 서비스를 하기 위한 중계 지점이 추가되는 한 결코 완성되지 않을 것이다.

sheer 　　완전한, 순전한

* The nervous anticipation as you're strapped into your seat, the questioning and regret that comes as you go up, up, up, and the sheer adrenaline rush as the car takes that first dive.

  당신이 좌석에서 안전벨트를 맬 때의 초조한 기대감, 당신이 높이, 높이 그리도 높이 올라갈 때 오는 의문과 후회, 그리고 차가 첫 번째 하강할 때 몰려드는 완전한 아드레날린.

shoplift
가게 물건을 훔치다

* A man who shoplifted from the Woolworth's store in Shanton in 1952 recently sent the shop an anonymous letter of apology.
1952년 쉔톤에 있는 울월스의 가게에서 물건을 훔친 한 남자가 최근에 그 가게에 익명의 반성문을 보냈다.

shorthand
속기, 약칭

* Even language is shorthand for the sense of belonging together, of sharing the same memories, the same historical experience, and the same cultural and imaginative heritage.
심지어 언어는 서로 속해 있다는 유대감, 동일한 기억의 공유, 동일한 역사적 경험, 동일한 문화적 / 창의적인 유산을 위한 속기이다.

shove
(거칠게) 밀치다[떠밀다], 아무렇게나 놓다[넣다]

* Eventually, you may shove or kick the door.
결국, 너는 문을 거칠게 밀치거나 찰 것이다.

significant
(영향을 주거나 두드러질 정도로) 중요한[의미 있는/커다란]

* In Locke's defense of private property, the significant point is what happens when we mix our labor with God's land.
사유재산에 대한 로크의 방어에 따르면 중요한 요점은 우리가 신이 내려준 토지에 우리의 노동이 결합할 때 무엇인가가 발생하느냐이다.

* They were indeed similar since they were both surprise attacks that drew America into significant wars.
그것들은 둘 다 미국을 심각한 전쟁으로 몰아 넣은 기습 공격이었기 때문에 정말로 비슷했다.

* The study, done by researchers from the University of California at San Francisco, revealed there was no significant change in the numbers of the restaurants that lost business before and after the pass of the laws.
그 연구는, 샌프란시스코의 캘리포니아 대학 연구자들에 의해 행해졌는데, 그 법의 통과되기 전후의 사업을 잃은 음식점들의 수에 의미 있는 변화가 없었다고 밝혀졌다.

sinus
부비강(두개골 속의, 코 안쪽으로 이어지는 구멍), 구멍

- Now that we've fixed your <u>sinuses</u>, we'll work on your other sense!
  이제 우리는 당신의 부비강을 고쳤으니, 다른 감각들도 치료할 거에요!

2008 하반기 지방직 9급

skirmish
(군대의, 특히 계획에 없던) 소규모 접전[충돌]

- He got a deadly wound inflicted in the <u>skirmish</u> with the well−trained enemy squad.
  그는 소규모 충돌에서 잘 훈련된 적의 부대에 의해 매우 치명적인 부상을 입었다.

snugly
아늑하게, 포근하게, 편안하게

- Ski masks cover their faces, woolen caps hide their hair, and heavy scarves are wrapped <u>snugly</u> around their necks.
  스키마스크는 그들의 얼굴을 덮고, 모직 모자는 그들의 머리를 가리고 두꺼운 스카프는 그들의 목을 포근하게 감싼다.

2012 상반기 지방직 9급

sobriety
술에 취하지 않은 상태, 맨 정신, 냉철함, 진지함

- The commander of this ship ought to command the ship's course and also command the justice, peace and <u>sobriety</u> both among the seamen and all the passengers.
  이 배의 사령관은 배의 항로를 지휘하고 또한 선원들과 모든 승객들 사이에서 정의, 평화 그리고 절제 된 행동을 지시해야 한다.

2010 행정안전부 9급, 2006 중앙인사위원회 9급

solely
혼자서, 단독으로, 아주, 오직

- Educated <u>solely</u> in the art of combat, these soldiers turned out to be the best fighters in the whole empire and shamelessly attacked the villages inhabited by their real families.
  단지 전투 기술만을 교육받은 이 군사들은 전 제국의 최고의 군인으로 탈바꿈했고, 뻔뻔스럽게도 그들의 가족이 사는 마을을 공격했다.

- Transient insomnia occurs <u>solely</u> due to an inadequate sleep environment.
  일시적 불면증은 오로지 적절치 않은 수면 환경 때문에 발생한다.

solitary
혼자 하는, 혼자 있기를 좋아하는

* Usually several skunks live together; however, adult male striped skunks are solitary during the summer.
일반적으로 수 십 마리의 스컹크들이 함께 모여서 산다. 그러나 성장한 수컷 줄무늬 스컹크들은 여름 동안 혼자 지낸다.

* But he also believed that creativity is rarely a solitary process but something brought out by social interactions.
그러나 그는 또한 창의성이 유일한 과정이 아니며 사회적인 상호작용에 의해 일어나는 어떤 것이라고 믿었다.

squeeze
쥐어짜다, 짜내다

* When faced with an intruder, the Camponotus cylindricus ant of Borneo will grab onto the invader and squeeze itself until it explodes.
Borneo의 Camponotus cylindricus 개미는 불법 침입자와 마주쳤을 때 침입자를 잡고 스스로 폭발할 때까지 쥐어 짤 것이다.

steady
안정된, 꾸준한, 변함없는, 한결같은

* The work is steady and the hours are good.
그 직업은 안정적이고 시간이 좋다.

stock
혈통, 종족, 주식, 재고품, 저장

* Perhaps less well known is the fact that there exist several racial stocks, such as the African Bushman and the Polynesians of the South Pacific, that do not fit any one racial classification but have characteristics of several races.
아마도 덜 알려진 것은 아프리카의 부시맨과 남태평양의 폴리네시아인들과 같은 여러 인종의 혈통이 존재한다는 사실인데, 이러한 인종들은 어떤 하나의 인종 분류에 맞지 않고 여러 인종의 특징을 가지고 있다.

* One way to face loss is with the perspective of a stock trader.
손실에 직면하는 한 가지 방식은 주식 거래자의 관점을 갖는 것이다.

strand

(실 · 전선 · 머리카락 등의) 가닥[올/줄], (생각 · 계획 · 이야기 등의) 가닥 [부분]

* The particles slice through <u>strands</u> of DNA, boosting the risk of cancer and other ailments.

  그 입자는 DNA의 가닥을 쉽게 통과하여 암이나 다른 질병의 피해를 북돋는다.

* It would be impossible to disentangle <u>strands</u> of influence in the spaghetti western, samurai film, Hollywood action flick, Indian adventure story, and Hong Kong cinema.

  서양의 스파게티, 사무라이 영화, 할리우드 액션영화, 인도의 모험담, 그리고 홍콩 영화에 미친 요소들을 구분하는 것은 불가능할 것이다.

strife

(개인 · 집단 간의) 갈등, 불화, (모든 종류의) 문제

* The increased power of the trade unions during and after the war not only intensified industrial <u>strife</u> but also meant that wage cuts were slower than price cuts.

  전쟁 전후로 증가한 무역조합의 힘은 개인의 갈등을 강화했을 뿐만 아니라, 감봉이 가격인하보다 더 천천히 이루어지게 했다.

subliminal

알지 못하는 사이 영향을 미치는

* At such short durations of exposure—known as <u>subliminal</u> exposurepeople cannot register the stimuli and hence, participants in the experiment were not expected to recall seeing the ideograms.

  그런 짧은 노출 지속 기간에-알지 못하게 일어나는 노출로 알려진- 사람들은 그 자극을 인식할 수 없었고, 이런 이유로 그 실험의 참가자들은 그 표의문자들을 본 것을 상기할 수 없었다.

subsidy

보조금

* During both World Wars, government <u>subsidies</u> and demands for new airplanes vastly improved techniques for their design and construction.

  두 차례의 세계 대전 동안 정부 보조금과 새로운 항공기에 대한 수요가 그 설계와 구조의 기술을 대단히 발전시켰다.

subtlety — 미묘함, 교묘함, 절묘함, 중요한 세부 요소[사항]들

* However, this precision cannot be achieved without real appreciation of the subtleties of language.
  그러나 이 정확성은 언어의 중요한 세부 요소들의 진정한 공감 없이는 성취될 수 없다.

suburbia — 교외, 교외 풍의 생활 양식

* Like squirrels and robins, white-tailed deer have adapted quite nicely to life on the edge of suburbia.
  다람쥐, 개똥지빠귀와 같이 흰 꼬리사슴은 살기 위해 도시 교외의 변두리 생활방식에 꽤 잘 적응하였다.

succession — 연속, (일정한 패턴을 이루는) 연쇄, 승계, 승계권

* We did it by collectively inventing a succession of what we have been calling wealth systems.
  우리는 부의 시스템이라고 불러왔던 하나의 연쇄를 집합적으로 발명함으로써 그것을 해냈다.

suffering — 고통

* Lewis Alfred Ellison, died in 1916 after an operation to cure internal wounds suffering after shards from a 100-lb ice block penetrated his abdomen when it was dropped while being loaded into a hopper.
  Lewis Alfred Ellison은 1916년 100파운드짜리 얼음 덩어리가 호퍼로 운반되는 도중 그것이 떨어져 그 얼음의 날카로운 부분이 그의 복부를 관통하여 고통 받다가 내부 상처를 치료하기 위한 수술을 받은 후 사망하였다.

sufficient — 충분한

* In fact, just being the first stimulus in a moderately repetitive series appears to be sufficient to induce subjective time expansion.
  사실, 단순히 반복되는 일련의 첫 번째 자극이 되는 것은 주관적 시간 확장을 유도하기에 충분한 것처럼 보인다.

supplant
(특히 낡거나 구식이 된 것을) 대신[대체]하다

* Their office work has largely been <u>supplanted</u> by the use of a computer program that fulfills the same function.
  그들의 사무업무는 주로 같은 기능을 수행하는 컴퓨터 프로그램의 사용으로 대체되어 왔다.

surreptitious
은밀한

* The audio of the <u>surreptitious</u> recording clearly indicates that the participants did not want to be recorded.
  은밀하게 녹음된 소리는 참가자들이 녹음되는 것을 원치 않는다는 것을 명백히 보여주었다.

surrogate
대리자

* Some of the newest laws authorize people to appoint a <u>surrogate</u> who can make medical decisions for them when necessary.
  새로운 법안 중 일부는 사람들이 필요할 때 그들을 위해 의학적 결정을 내려 줄 대리인을 임명할 수 있도록 권한을 부여한다.

susceptible
민감한, (감수성이) 예민한, ~을 허용 할 수 있는

* One bacterium that survives keeps replicating because it is not <u>susceptible</u> to the drug treatment.
  살아남는 하나의 박테리아는 약물요법에 민감하기 때문에 계속하여 복제한다

suspend
매달다, (공식적으로) 중단하다, 연기하다, 정학[정직]시키다

* Passive euthanasia means letting a patient die for lack of treatment or <u>suspending</u> treatment that has begun.
  수동적 안락사는 환자를 치료하지 않거나, 계속해왔던 치료를 지연시키면서 죽도록 내버려두는 것을 의미한다.
* Sesta has <u>suspended</u> a new car project.
  Sesta는 신 차 프로젝트를 중단하였다.

sustain

지속시키다. 지속하게 하다

- Some movies explored the possibility of <u>sustaining</u> human life in outer space.
어떤 영화들이 우주 바깥에 인간의 삶을 지속하는 가능성을 탐구했다.

swath

(목초·보리 등의) 한 번 낫질한 자취, 한 번 벤 목초, 넓은 길, 긴 행렬, (항해) 물결의 폭

- In one of the most widespread man—made disasters the region has known, smoke from the fires has blanketed a broad <u>swath</u> of Southeast Asia this month.
널리 알려진 인재 중의 하나로 알려져 온, 그 화재의 연기가 이번 달 동남아시아의 넓은 길을 뒤덮었다.

taint

(평판 등을) 더럽히다, 오점[오명]을 남기다

- Few words are <u>tainted</u> by so much subtle nonsense and confusion as profit.
영리만큼 그렇게나 미묘한 얼토당토않은 말과 혼란에 의해 더럽혀진 단어는 거의 없다.

tantalizing

애타게 하는, 감질나게 하는

- <u>Tantalizing</u> offers like these from your credit—card issuers are increasingly filled with traps that can pile on unexpected fees or trigger punitive interest, as high as 35%.
당신의 신용카드 발행자들로부터의 이와 같은 감질나는 제안들은 점점 예기치 않은 요금을 쌓거나 35%나 되는 높은 가혹한 이자를 유발 할 수 있는 덫들로 채워졌다.

tentative

잠정적인, 자신 없는

- The company and the union reached a <u>tentative</u> agreement in this year s wage deal as the two sides took the company's deteriorating operating profits seriously amid unfriendly business environments.
노사는 양쪽 모두 사업 환경이 좋지 않은 가운데 회사의 영업 이익 악화를 심각하게 받아들이면서 올해 임금 협상에서 잠정적인 합의에 도달했다.

term   (특정한 이름으로) 칭하다, 불리다

- One well-known difficulty in finding new things has been <u>termed</u> the 'oasis trap' by the cognitive psychologist David Perkins.

  새로운 것들을 찾을 때 한 가지 잘 알려진 어려움은 인지심리학자인 David Perkins에 의해 'oasis trap'이라고 명명되었다.

thesauruses   유의어 사전

- These web sites offer multiple resources (<u>thesauruses</u>, encyclopedias, and quotation guides, to name a few)

  이 웹사이트들은 다양한 자료를 제공한다. (몇 개만 예를 들자면 유의어 사전, 백과사전, 인용서)

thoroughly   철저하게

- If you wanted to stay healthy, you could wash your hands, boil your water, cook your food <u>thoroughly</u>, and clean cuts and scrapes with iodine.

  건강을 유지하기를 원한다면, 손을 씻거나, 물을 끓이거나, 음식을 철저하게 조리하거나 베인 상처와 긁힌 상처를 요오드 용액으로 깨끗이 할 수 있다.

tidbit   맛있는 가벼운 음식, (맛있는 것의) 한 입, 재미있는 이야기, 토막 뉴스

- After supper, with more spilled milk, uneaten vegetables and <u>tidbits</u> fed to the cat under the table, it's finally time for bed.

  더욱 흘려진 우유와 먹지 않은 야채들, 식탁 밑에 있는 고양이에게 먹여진 가벼운 음식들과 함께한 저녁식사 후에, 마침내 잠자리에 들 시간이 온다.

tolerance   관용, 아량, 포용력, 공평함, 인내(력)

- 'Zero <u>tolerance</u>' is a phrase that first came to light as a description of the crackdown on trivial crime.

  '무관용'은 사소한 범죄에 대한 엄중 단속의 묘사로 처음 알려진 관용구이다.

2018 인사혁신처

tolerate   인내하다

* In addition, good listeners are inclined to accept or <u>tolerate</u> rather than to judge and criticize.
  게다가 남의 말을 잘 듣는 사람들은 판단하거나 비판하는 것보다는 차라리 받아들이거나 인내하는 경향이 있다.

2007 행정자치부 9급

top-notch   (비 격식) 최고의, 아주 뛰어난

* He's really <u>top-notch</u> administrator.
  그는 정말로 뛰어난 이사다.

2017 제2회 서울특별시 9급

transient   일시적인, 순간적인

* Prudence indeed will dictate that governments long established should not be changed for light and <u>transient</u> causes.
  사실상, 신중함은 오래전에 설립된 정부가 사소하고 일시적인 원인으로 변경될 수 없다는 것을 암시할 것이다.

2017 인사혁신처

transmit   전송하다

* Since the optic nerve contains roughly eighteen times as many neurons as the cochlear nerve, we assume it <u>transmits</u> at least that much more information.
  시신경이 달팽이관 신경보다 약 18배 많은 뉴런을 포함하고 있기 때문에, 우리는 눈이 더 많은 정보를 전달한다고 추정한다.

2016 인사혁신처 9급

tremendous   거대한, 엄청난, 굉장한

* Character is, above all, a <u>tremendous</u> humility before the facts—an automatic alliance with truth even when that truth is bitter medicine.
  무엇보다도 인격이란 사실 앞에서의 거대한 겸허함이며, 심지어 진실이 쓴 약인 상황에서도 그 진실에 대한 조건반사적인 협력이다.
* Some seniors experience a <u>tremendous</u> loss of self − esteem.
  몇몇 노인들은 엄청난 자부심의 상실을 경험한다.

2018 제1회 서울특별시 9급

trigger   계기, 도화선

* The <u>trigger</u> for the aggressive driver is usually traffic congestion coupled with a schedule that is almost impossible to meet.
난폭 운전자의 계기는 보통 충족시키기 거의 불가능한 일정과 겹친 교통 혼잡이다.

2011 행정안전부 9급

unashamedly   염치없이

* Character implies the ability to laugh wholeheartedly and weep <u>unashamedly</u>.
캐릭터는 진정으로 웃거나 부끄러움 없이 우는 능력을 시사한다.

2017 인사혁신처

uncanny   이상한, 묘한

* I had an <u>uncanny</u> feeling that I had seen this scene somewhere before.
나는 내가 이 장면을 이전에 어디선가 본 것 같은 이상한 감정을 느꼈다.

2012 행정안전부 9급

uncover   덮개를 벗기다, 뚜껑을 열다, (비밀 등을) 알아내다

* The use of questions can <u>uncover</u> distortions and clarify misunderstandings.
질문의 사용은 왜곡된 부분을 확인하고 오해된 부분을 분명히 할 수 있다.

2017 제2회 서울특별시 9급

unhelpful   도움이 되지 않는

* Definitions are especially <u>unhelpful</u> to children.
정의는 특별히 아이들에게 도움이 되지 않는다.

2012 행정안전부 9급

unnameable   이름 붙일 수 없는, 말할 수 없는

* Money and power do not satisfy that <u>unnameable</u> hunger in the soul.
돈과 권력은 영혼의 명명할 수 없는 갈구를 충족시킬 수 없다.

2016 인사혁신처 9급

unprecedented
전례없는, 미증유의

- Newton made unprecedented contributions to mathematics, optics, and mechanical physics.
  뉴턴은 수학, 광학, 기계물리학에 전례 없는 기여를 했다.

2015 사회복지직 9급

vapor
(공기 중의 수증기 · 김 · 안개 · 운무 등) 증기, 허황된 생각, 우울증

- Warm air can hold more water vapor than cold air.
  따뜻한 공기는 차가운 공기보다 더 많은 수증기를 수용할 수 있다.

- Thus, water vapor could be much less likely to turn to rain without the dust particles.
  그러므로 수증기는 먼지 입자 없이 비로 변할 가능성이 많이 적어진다.

2018 제1회 서울특별시 9급

verbal
말로 된, 구두의

- Mephisto demands a signature and contract. No mere verbal contract will do.
  Mephisto는 서명과 계약을 요구하고 있다. 단지 구두 계약으로는 충분하지 않을 것이다.

2013 안정행정부, 2012 행정안전부 9급

verify
(진실인지 · 정확한지) 확인하다, 입증하다

- That's why the active listener verifies completeness by asking questions.
  그것이 바로 능동적인 청자가 질문을 함으로써 완성도를 확인한 이유이다.

2011 행정안전부 9급

viability
(특히 태아 · 신생아의) 생육[생존] 능력, (계획 등의) 실행 가능성

- The viability of reclaimed water for indirect potable reuse should be assessed with regard to quantity and reliability of raw water supplies, the quality of reclaimed water, and cost effectiveness.
  2차적인 식수로서 재활용 재생수를 사용할 수 있는가의 문제는 상수의 양과 신뢰도, 재생수의 질, 그리고 비용 효율성에 관련하여 평가되어야 한다.

vibrant 활기찬, 선명한

* For centuries, people gazing at the sky after sunset could see thousands of <u>vibrant</u>, sparkling stars.
  수 세기 동안 해가 진 뒤 하늘을 응시하는 사람들은 선명하게 반짝이는 수 천 개의 별들을 볼 수 있었다.

versatile 다용도의, 다재다능한

* Kohlrabi is delicious, <u>versatile</u> and good for you.
  콜라비는 맛있고, 다용도이고 당신에게 유익하다.

vehicle 수송 수단, 탈것, 매개물, 전달 수단

* We could see that a truck had been involved in the accident and knew it would take some time to move the <u>vehicles</u> to the side of the road.
  우리는 한 트럭이 교통사고를 낸 것을 볼 수 있었고 사고 차량들을 갓길로 옮기는 데 약간의 시간이 걸릴 거라는 것을 알았다.

* A growing body of research by automakers is finding that buyers of these two kinds of <u>vehicles</u> are very different psychologically.
  자동차 제조업자들이 행한 고조되는 일련의 연구는 이 두 종류의 자동차 구매자들이 심리적으로 매우 다르다는 것을 발견하고 있다.

* The one thing that all these cycles have in common is that they are all self-propelled, two-wheeled <u>vehicles</u>.
  이 모든 오토바이의 한 가지 공통점은 그것들 모두 자체 추진력이 있고 두 개의 바퀴가 달린 탈것이라는 점이다.

veteran (어떤 분야의) 베테랑, 참전 용사

* Another interesting result was found when <u>veteran</u> detergent customers were not shown the box, and were asked to choose their favorite brand based only on the result of the detergent.
  그 박스를 보여주지 않고 오직 세정력의 결과만을 기초로 하여 그들이 선호하는 브랜드를 선택하도록 요청받은 베테랑 세정제 고객들로부터 또 다른 흥미로운 결과가 발견되었다.

| **warp** | (원래의 모습을 잃고) 휘대[틀어지다], (행동 등을) 비뚤어지게만들다 |

- But I seemed to slip into a time warp when I visited Morrie, and I like myself better when I was there.
  그러나 나는 시간 왜곡으로 미끄러져 들어가는 것처럼 보였고, 나는 나 자신을 내가 그곳에 있었을 때보다 더 좋아했다.

| **whimper** | 훌쩍이다, 훌쩍이며 말하다, 훌쩍거림 |

- But then, as lonely males sought fruitlessly for mates, it may have simply faded away, with a whimper.
  하지만 그때, 외로운 수컷들은 아무런 결실 없이 짝을 찾아 다녔고, 그것(공룡)은 훌쩍이며 사라져갔을 것이다.

| **wholeheartedly** | 진심으로, 착실하게, 진정으로, 전적으로 |

- Character implies the ability to laugh wholeheartedly and weep unashamedly.
  캐릭터는 진정으로 웃거나 부끄러움 없이 우는 능력을 시사한다.

2005년부터 2019년까지 국가직 · 지방직 공무원시험에서 출제되었던 단어 중 다시 출제될 가능성이 높은 단어들을 선별하여 기출단어로 수록하였습니다. 영영뜻을 통해 어휘의 보다 정확한 의미를 이해할 수 있습니다.

LESSON

02

기출단어
(영영뜻)

2006 서울시 9급

abate

■ (폭풍·추위 등이) 누그러지다, 약해지다, (수·양·정도 등을) 줄이다

to become less strong or decrease

Example We waited for the storm to _____.

📄 abate

2015 인사혁신처 9급, 2013 안정행정부 9급·국회사무처

ability

■ 할수있음, 능력

Your ability to do something is the fact that you can do it.

2014 제1회 지방직 9급, 2006 서울시 9급

abolish

■ (제도·법률·습관 등을) 폐지하다

to officially end a law, system, etc., especially one that has existed for a long time

2006 중앙인사위원회 9급

abortion

■ 낙태, 인공 유산(=termination), 자연 유산(=miscarriage), (계획 등의) 실패

a medical operation to end a pregnancy so that the baby is not born alive

2006 서울시 9급

abrade

■ 문질러 벗겨지게[닳게] 하다, 닳다, 벗겨지다

to rub something so hard that the surface becomes damaged

2015 제1회 지방직 9급, 2014 안전행정부 9급

absolutely

■ 절대적으로, 무조건으로, 정말로

completely and in every way ; used to emphasize something

2013 제1회 지방직

absorb

■ 흡수하다

It soaks it up or takes it in. (a liquid, gas, or other substance)

It takes it in. (light, heat, or another form of energy)

2006 중앙선거관리위원회 9급

accepted

■ 인정되는, 받아들여지는

considered right or suitable by most people

access	2014 안전행정부 9급

access 접근, 면회, 이용[출입] 권리, 통로

the right to enter a place, use something, see someone, etc. ; how easy or difficult it is for people to enter a public building, to reach a place, or talk to someone ; the way you use to enter a building or reach a place

2014 안전행정부 9급

accomplish 이루다, 성취하다, 완수하다

to succeed in doing something, especially after trying very hard

2014 사회복지직 9급, 2007 행정자치부 9급

accumulation 축적, 누적, 재산, (대학에서 높은 학위와 낮은 학위를) 동시 취득하기

an amount of something that has been collected

2010 서울특별시 9급

accurate 정확한, 틀림없는(↔ inaccurate)

correct and true in every detail ; measured or calculated correctly

2011 상반기 지방직 9급

acquisition 습득, 구입[취득]한 것, (기업)인수, 매입

something that someone buys, often to add to a collection of things

2013 서울시 9급

acute 날카로운, 예리한, 격렬한, 극심한, 예민한

an acute problem is very serious ; an acute feeling is very strong ; an acute illness or disease quickly becomes very serious ; acute senses such as hearing, taste, touch, etc. are very good and sensitive

2013 안전행정부 · 사회복지직 9급

adapt ~을 적응시키다, 순응시키다, (건물 · 기계 등을 용도에 맞추어) 개조하다, (소설 · 극을) 개작하다, 각색하다

to gradually change your behavior and attitudes in order to be successful in a new situation ; to change something to make it suitable for a different purpose ; if a book or play is adapted for film, television, etc., it is changed so that it can be made into a film, television programme, etc.

2005 서울시 9급

addictive (약물 등이) 중독성의, (활동 등이) 중독성이 있는

If a drug is addictive, people who take it cannot stop taking it.

adequate	2014 제1회 지방직 9급, 2011 법원행정처 9급

adequate

충분한, 알맞은, 적당한

enough in quantity or of a good enough quality for a particular purpose ; fairly good but not excellent

2009 행정안전부 9급

adjunct

부속물, 부가물

something that is joined or added to another thing but is not an essential part of it

2012 상반기 지방직 9급, 2006 중앙선거관리위원회 9급

adopt

채용하다, 채택하다

to formally approve a proposal, amendment, etc., especially by voting ; to choose a new name, country, custom, etc., especially to replace a previous one

2005 대구시 9급

adornment

꾸미기, 장식, 장식품

something that you use to decorate something ; the act of decorating something

2006 서울시 9급

adventurous

대담한, 모험적인, 모험을 좋아하는, 위험한

not afraid of taking risks or trying new things ; eager to go to new places and do exciting or dangerous things

2006 대구광역시 9급, 2005 국회사무처 8급

adversity

역경, 불운, 불행, 재난

a situation in which you have a lot of problems that seem to be caused by bad luck

2012 상반기 지방직 9급

advocate

주창자, 창도자, 대변자, 중재자, 변호사

someone who publicly supports someone or something ; a lawyer who speaks in a court of law, especially in Scotland

 Example She's a passionate _____ of natural childbirth.

📘 advocated

2014 법원사무직 9급, 2013 안전행정부, 2006 · 2005 중앙인사위원회 9급

affect

~에 영향을 미치다

to do something that produces an effect or change in something or in someone's situation ; to make someone feel strong emotions

affection
2011 기상청 9급, 2009 행정안전부 9급

애정, 호의, 감동, 감정, 영향

a feeling of liking or love and caring ; somebody's affections the feelings of love and caring that someone has

affordable
2010 행정안전부 9급

줄 수 있는, 입수 가능한, (가격이) 알맞은, 감당할 수 있는 물건[비용]

to be able to pay for something, to supply or provide something needed or wanted to someone

aggression
2008 상반기 지방직 9급

공격성, 공격, 침략

angry or violent behavior or feelings

aggravate
2013 안전행정부 9급

(질병이나 좋지 못한 상황을) 악화시키다

If someone or something aggravates a situation, they make it worse.

ailing
2005 중앙인사위원회 9급

병든, 앓고 있는, 괴로워하는, (회사·경제가) 침체한

ill and not likely to get better ; an ailing company, organization, or economy is having a lot of problems and is not successful

ailment
2007 행정자치부 9급, 2006 중앙인사위원회 9급

병, 불쾌

an illness that is not very serious

alert
2014 법원사무직 9급

방심하지 않는, 조심하는, 기민한, 민첩한

giving all your attention to what is happening, being said, etc. ; able to think quickly and clearly

alias
2006 서울시 9급

별명, 가명

a false name, usually used by a criminal

alienate
2009 행정안전부 9급

(사람을) 멀어지게 만들다, 소외감을 느끼게 하다

to make someone unfriendly

alignment
2008 하반기 지방직 9급

가지런함, (정치적) 지지

place or arrange in a straight line or into correct relative positions

aloft
2012 행정안전부 9급
하늘[위로] 높이
up in or into the air

alternate
2015 인사혁신처 9급, 2013 제1회 지방직 9급, 2005 국회사무처 8급
번갈아 일어나다, 교체하다, 교차하다
if two things alternate, or if you alternate them, they happen one after the other in a repeated pattern

alternative
2015 인사혁신처 9급
둘(때로 셋 이상) 중의 하나, 양자택일, 대안
something you can choose to do or use instead of something else

altogether
2015 인사혁신처 9급, 2014 제1회 지방직 9급
대체로, 완전히, 전혀, 모두, 통틀어
used to emphasize that something has been done completely or has finished completely ; used to emphasize that the way you describe something is completely true ; used to show that you are referring to the total amount ; used to make a final statement about several things you have just mentioned

amass
2005 국회사무처 8급
~을 모으다, 축적하다
if you amass money, knowledge, information, etc., you gradually collect a large amount of it

 For 25 years, Darwin _____ evidence to support his theories.

☑ amassed

amendment
2007 행정자치부 9급, 2005 국회사무처 8급
(법안·헌법 등의) 수정(안), 개정(안)
a small change, improvement, or addition that is made to a law or document, or the process of doing this

anabolic
2010 행정안전부 9급
동화작용의
a hormone (= chemical made by living cells) that causes muscle and bone growth

analyze	2009 상반기 지방직 9급 분석하다, 분해하다, 검토하다 to examine or think about something carefully, in order to understand it ; to examine a substance to see what it is made of ; to examine someone's mental or emotional problems by using psychoanalysis
ancestral	2015 인사혁신처 9급, 2011 상반기 지방직 9급 조상의, 조상 전래의, 원형을 이루는 a person, typically one more remote than a grandparent, from whom one is descended
ancient	2015 인사혁신처 9급, 2014 법원사무직 9급, 2010 상반기 지방직 9급 고대의, 옛날의, 예로부터의 belonging to a time long ago in history, especially thousands of years ago ; having existed for a very long time ; very old — used humorously
anguish	2012 상반기 지방직 9급 (극심한) 괴로움, 비통 severe mental or physical pain or suffering
anniversary	2014 안전행정부 9급 기념일, 기념제 a date on which something special or important happened in a previous year
annoy	2015 사회복지직 9급, 2014 법원사무직 9급, 2013 서울특별시 9급 괴롭히다, 귀찮게 하다 to make someone feel slightly angry and unhappy about something
anonymity	2011 상반기 지방직 9급 익명, 무명, 작자 불명, 정체불명의 인물 when other people do not know who you are or what your name is
antibody	2012 행정안전부 9급 항체 a blood protein produced by the body in response to and counteracting an antigen
anticipate	2006 중앙인사위원회 9급 예상하다, 기대하다, 미리 걱정하다 to expect that something will happen and be ready for it
anti-inflammatory	2008 하반기 지방직 9급 소염제[항염증제]인 used to control or reduce inflammation

antipathy

2006 중앙선거관리위원회 9급

반감, 혐오(감)(=dislike, aversion)

a feeling of strong dislike towards someone or something

apparent

2014 안전행정부 9급, 2006 중앙인사위원회 9급

분명한

easy to notice

 Example It soon became _____ that we had a major problem.

답 apparent

appeal

2014 안전행정부 9급, 2012 상반기 지방직 9급

간청하다, 애원하다

to make a serious public request for help, money, information, etc. ; to make a formal request to a court or someone in authority asking for a decision to be changed

application

2011 기상청 9급, 2006 서울시 9급

적용, 응용, 신청, 지원

practical purpose for which a machine, idea, etc. can be used, or a situation when this is used ; a formal, usually written, request for something such as a job, place at university, or permission to do something

Example We receive hundreds of job _____ each year.

답 applications

appoint

2015 제1회 지방직 9급, 2012 하반기 지방직 9급

임명하다, 임용하다

to choose someone for a position or a job

appreciate

2013 안전행정부

감사하다, 감상하다, 높이 평가하다, 올바르게 인식하다

to understand how serious or important a situation or problem is or what someone's feelings are ; used to thank someone in a polite way or to say that you are grateful for something they have done ; to understand how good or useful someone or something is

appropriate	2015 제1회 지방직 9급, 2011 행정안전부 9급 적당한, 알맞은, 특유한, 고유한 correct or suitable for a particular time, situation, or purpose
approve	2014 사회복지직 9급, 2005 국회사무처 8급 승인하다, 비준하다, 인정하다 to officially accept a plan, proposal, etc. ; to think that someone or something is good, right, or suitable
archaeological	2006 서울시 9급 고고학의 relating to archaeology
ardent	2005 국회사무처 8급 열렬한, 열심인, 불타는 듯한 showing strong positive feelings about an activity and determination to succeed at it ; showing strong feelings of love
aristocracy	2006 중앙인사위원회 9급 귀족, 귀족 사회, 귀족 정치 the people in the highest social class, who traditionally have a lot of land, money, and power
arrogant	2010 국회사무처 9급, 2006 서울시 9급 거만한, 거드름 부리는, 오만한 behaving in an unpleasant or rude way because you think you are more important than other people
artery	2014 법원사무직 9급 동맥, 주요 수로[도로], 간선, 중추 one of the tubes that carries blood from your heart to the rest of your body ; a main road, railway line, river, etc.
articulator	2008 상반기 지방직 9급 조음 기관(혀 · 입술 · 치아같이 소리를 내는 데 이용되는 입 속 기관), 발음이 또렷한 사람 any of the vocal organs above the larynx, including the tongue, lips, teeth, and hard palate
ascend	2012 상반기 지방직 9급 오르다, 올라가다 to move up or climb something
ascendant	2005 국회사무처 8급 우월한, 지배적인 ; 우위, 우월 becoming more powerful or popular

ascent	2005 국회사무처 8급 상승, 오름, 올라감, 향상 the act of climbing something or moving upwards ; the process of becoming more important, powerful, or successful than before
ashamed	2015 사회복지직 9급, 2011 행정안전부 9급, 2005 대구시 9급 부끄러워하는, 수줍어하는, 수치스러워하는 feeling embarrassed and guilty because of something you have done ; feeling uncomfortable because someone does something that embarrasses you
ashtray	2012 행정안전부 9급 재떨이 a small dish or containerin which people can leave cigarette ash and cigarette ends
aspect	2015 사회복지직 9급, 2014 사회복지직 9급, 2006 중앙인사위원회 9급 외관, 관점, 양상, 용모 one part of a situation, idea, plan, etc. that has many parts ; the appearance of someone or something
assault	2005 국회사무처 8급 비난, 폭행, (갑작스런) 습격 ; ~을 공격하다, 습격하다 a strong spoken or written criticism of someone else's ideas, plans, etc. ; the crime of physically attacking someone ; a military attack to take control of a place controlled by the enemy

Example He was jailed for _____.

答 assault

assessment	2005 중앙인사위원회 9급 평가 a process in which you make a judgment about a person or situation, or the judgment you make ; a calculation about the cost or value of something

Example What's Michael's _____ of the situation?

答 assessment

association

2015 인사혁신처 9급, 2005 대구시 9급

협회, 연합, 교제, 제휴, 연상, 함축

an organization that consists of a group of people who have the same aims, do the same kind of work, etc. ; a relationship with a particular person, organization, group, etc. ; a connection or relationship between two events, ideas, situations, etc. ; a feeling or memory that is related to a particular place, event, word, etc.

asthma

2014 서울시 9급, 2006 중앙인사위원회 9급

천식

a medical condition that causes difficulties in breathing

astronaut

2013 안전행정부 9급, 2010 국회사무처 9급

우주 비행사

someone who travels and works in a spacecraft

atavism

2011 상반기 지방직 9급

격세 유전

happening because of a very old natural and basic habit from the distant past, not because of a conscious decision or present need or usefulness

athlete

2014 제1차 순경, 2013 안전행정부

운동선수, 경기자

someone who competes in sports competitions, especially running, jumping, and throwing ; someone who is good at sports and who often does sports

athletic

2014 안전행정부 9급, 2005 대구시 9급

(운동) 경기의, 체육의, (체격이) 스포츠맨다운, 강건한

physically strong and good at sport ; relating to athletics

atmosphere

2015 사회복지직 9급, 2013 제1회 지방직 9급

대기, 공기, 기압, 환경, 주위의 상황, 분위기

the mixture of gases that surrounds the Earth ; the mixture of gases that surround a planet ; the feeling that an event or place gives you ; if a place or event has atmosphere, it is interesting

attach

2013 안전행정부

~에게 애착을 갖게 하다, 사모하게 하다(to), 붙이다, 달다

be attached to somebody/something to like someone or something very much, because you have known them or had them for a long time ; to fasten or connect one object to another

attitude	2013 서울특별시
	■ (사람 · 사물에 대한) 태도, 마음가짐, (사물에 대한) 사고방식, 의견, 자세
	the opinions and feelings that you usually have about something ; the way that you behave towards someone or in a particular situation, especially when this shows how you feel ; a style of dressing, behaving, etc. that shows you have the confidence to do unusual and exciting things without caring what other people think
audible	2010 행정안전부 9급
	■ 잘 들리는
	heard or able to be heard
augmentative	2011 행정안전부 9급
	■ 증가적인, 〈접사 또는 접사가 붙은 단어가〉어의를 확장하는
	expressing large size, intensity, or seniority
authority	2015 제1회 지방직 9급
	■ 권위, 권력, 당국
	a quality in the way you speak or behave which makes people obey you ; the power you have because of your official position ; the authorities the people or organizations that are in charge of a particular country or area
autism	2012 상반기 지방직 9급
	■ 자폐증
	a failure to develop social abilities, language and other communication skills to the usual level
autonomous	2015 서울특별시 9급
	■ 자치권이 있는, 자율의, 자주적인, 자발적인
	an autonomous place or organization is free to govern or control itself ; having the ability to work and make decisions by yourself without any help from anyone else
available	2015 사회복지직 9급, 2013 안전행정부
	■ 쓸모 있는, 유효한, 이용할 수 있는
	something that is available is able to be used or can easily be bought or found ; someone who is available is not busy and has enough time to talk to you

ban	2015 인사혁신처 9급, 2014 서울시 9급
	금지하다
	to say that something must not be done, seen, used, etc.
	Example Smoking is _____ in the building.
	답 banned

baneful	2010 상반기 지방직 9급
	사악한, 유독한, 파멸을 초래하는
	a cause of great distress or annoyance

barbarian	2006 중앙선거관리위원회 9급
	야만인, 미개인
	someone from a different tribe or land, who people believe to be wild and not civilized

bark	2010 행정안전부 9급
	나무껍질, 수피(=skin)
	the outer covering of a tree

batter	2010 행정안전부 9급
	난타하다, 강타하다, 때려 부수다, 포격하다
	to hit someone or something again and again, in a way that hurts someone or causes damage

beguiling	2011 상반기 지방직 9급
	묘한 매력이 있는
	charm or enchant

behave	2014 안전행정부 9급
	행동하다, (어린이가) 예절 바르게 행동하다
	to do things that are good, bad, sensible, etc. ; if something behaves in a particular way, it does those things ; to not do things that annoy or offend people

beneficial	2015 제1회 지방직 9급
	유익한, 이로운, (신탁 재산 등이) 수익권(受益權)이 있는
	having a good effect
	Example Cycling is highly _____ to health and the environment.
	답 beneficial

beneficiary	2014 사회복지직 9급, 2011 행정안전부 9급 수혜자, (유산)수령인 someone or something that benefits from something
benign	2008 하반기 지방직 9급 인자한, 상냥한, (운명·전조 등이) 길한, (기후 등이) 온화한 kind and gentle
bestow	2005 대구시 9급 주다, 수여하다, (시간·생각 등을) 사용하다, 바치다 to give someone something of great value or importance
bimonthly	2005 대구시 9급 2개월마다의, 격월의; 2개월마다, 격월로 appearing or happening every two months or twice each month
binoculars	2011 상반기 지방직 9급 쌍안경 an optical instrument with a lens for each eye, used for viewing distant objects
biology	2012 하반기 지방직 생물학 the scientific study of living things ; the scientific laws that control the life of a particular type of animal, plant, etc.
biometric	2006 중앙인사위원회 9급 생물 측정학의 relating to technology that can be used to measure things such as people's eyes or fingerprints. These measurements can be kept on computer and then used to check someone's identity, for example when they show a passport at an airport
biotech	2010 서울시 9급 생명 공학, 인간 공학(=biotechnology) the use of living things such as cells, bacteria, etc. to make drugs, destroy waste matter, etc.
biracial	2006 서울시 9급 두 인종으로 된, 혼혈의 representing or including people from two different races

blast furnace

2005 대구시 9급

용광로(=smelting[melting] furnace)

a large industrial structure in which iron is separated from the rock that surrounds it

blink

2005 대구시 9급

눈을 깜박거리다, 깜짝 놀라서 보다, 흘긋 보다

to shut and open your eyes quickly

blooper

2007 행정자치부 9급

(사람들 앞에서 범하는 당황스러운) 실수

an embarrassing mistake usually made in public

bluff

2012 상반기 지방직 9급

허세를 부리다, 엄포를 놓다, 허세, 엄포, (특히 바다나 강가의) 절벽

expression of self-confidence for the purpose of intimidation, rising steeply with a flat or rounded front

bounce

2014 법원사무직 9급

(공 등이) 튀다, 튀어 오르다, 벌떡 일어나다, 펄쩍 뛰다

if a ball or other object bounces, or you bounce it, it immediately moves up or away from a surface after hitting it ; to move up and down, especially because you are hitting a surface that is made of rubber, has springs, etc.

breakdown

2013 제1회 지방직 · 안전행정부

고장, 파손, 몰락(=downfall), (교섭 등의) 결렬, (정신 · 육체 등의) 쇠약

an occasion when a car or a piece of machinery breaks and stops working ; the failure of a relationship or system ; a serious medical condition in which someone becomes mentally ill and is unable to work or deal with ordinary situations in life

----

 A sudden rise in oil prices could lead to a _____ of the economy.

日 breakdown

----

bureau

2012 하반기 지방직, 2008 하반기 지방직 9급

(보통 뚜껑을 여닫을 수 있는) 책상, (특정 주제에 대한 정보를 제공하는) 사무실[단체], (미국 정부의) 부서[국]

a piece of furniture with several drawers, a government department in the U.S., an office or organization that provides services or information to the public

bureaucracy

관료 정치[주의, 제도], (집합적) 관료

a complicated official system which is annoying or confusing because it has a lot of rules, processes, etc. ; the officials who are employed rather than elected to do the work of a government, business, etc.

bulge

2016 서울특별시 9급

가득 차다, 불룩하다

If something such as a person's stomach bulges, it sticks out.

bury

2005 대구시 9급

묻다, 파묻다

to put someone who has died in a grave ; to put something under the ground, often in order to hide it

bush

2005 대구시 9급

관목(=shrub), 덤불

a plant with many thin branches growing up from the ground

bygone

2010 상반기 지방직 9급

과거의 ; 과거(의 일)

bygone age/era/days, etc. a period of time in the past

calculate

2013 안전행정부, 2006 서울시 9급

계산하다, 추산하다, 추정하다, 평가하다

to find out how much something will cost, how long something will take, etc., by using numbers ; to guess something using as many facts as you can find

candidate

2007 국회사무처 8급, 2006 중앙인사위원회 9급

후보자

someone who is being considered for a job or is competing in an election

Example There are only three _____ for the job.

candidates

candor

2009 행정안전부 9급

공평무사, 허심탄회, 솔직, 정직, 순백

the quality of being honest and telling the truth, especially about a difficult or embarrassing subject

canine	개, 개의, 송곳니
	relating to dogs, the pointy tooth between the incisors and the premolars
capital	자본, 자산, 수도, 대문자
	money or property, especially when it is used to start a business or to produce more wealth ; an important city where the main government of a country, state, etc. is ; a letter of the alphabet written in its large form as it is, for example, at the beginning of someone's name
capitalism	자본주의
	an economic and political system in which businesses belong mostly to private owners, not to the government
captive	포로의, 포로가 된, 사로잡힌
	kept in prison or in a place that you are not allowed to leave
carbon dioxide	이산화탄소
	the gas produced when animals breathe out, when carbon is burned in air, or when animal or vegetable substances decay
carefully	주의 깊게, 조심스럽게, 신중히
	in a careful way
carnage	대학살
	the violent killing of large numbers of people, especially in war
castes	계급
	one of the classes into which the Hindu people of India were traditionally divided, a division of society based upon differences of wealth, rank, or occupation
celestial	하늘의, 천체의, 천상의
	relating the sky

cellular phone

2013 안전행정부

휴대폰(=mobile phone)

a telephone that you can carry with you and use in any place

charm

2015 사회복지직 9급, 2005 대구시 9급

부적, 매력, 마력, 주문

a special quality someone or something has that makes people like them, feel attracted to them, or be easily influenced by them — used to show approval ; a phrase or action believed to have special magic powers

chemical

2013 안전행정부

화학 물질 ; 화학의, 화학 작용의

a substance used in chemistry or produced by a chemical process ; relating to substances, the study of substances, or processes involving changes in substances

chromosome

2006 중앙인사위원회 9급

염색체

a part of every living cell that is shaped like a thread and contains the genes that control the size, shape, etc. that a plant or animal has

chunk

2005 대구시 9급

큰 덩어리, 상당한 양[액수]

a large thick piece of something that does not have an even shape ; a large part or amount of something

circumlocution

2011 행정안전부 9급

(격식)에둘러[우회적으로] 말하기

an indirect way of saying something

circumscribe

2012 상반기 지방직 9급

(권리 · 자유 등을) 제한[억제]하다, ~의 둘레에 선을 긋다

to limit something, to draw a circle which surrounds it and tou—ches each of its corners

civic

2013 서울특별시, 2005 대구시 9급

시의, 도시의, 시민의

relating to a town or city ; relating to the people who live in a town or city

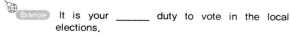

It is your _____ duty to vote in the local elections.

답 civic

civilized
교화된, 문명화한, 문명인[국]의
a civilized society is well organized and developed, and has fair laws and customs

clamor
2005 국회사무처 8급
큰 외침소리, 절규, 야유
a very loud noise made by a large group of people or animals ; the expression of feelings of anger and shock by a large number of people — used especially in news reports

clearly
2012 상반기 지방직 9급, 2006 서울시 9급
(문장 전체를 수식하여) 분명히, 의심할 여지없이
without any doubt

clutter
2008 하반기 지방직 9급
(너무 많은 것들을 어수선하게) 채우다[집어넣다], 잡동사니, 어수선함
a lot of objects in a state of being untidy

cog
2005 국회사무처 8급
(톱니바퀴의) 톱니, 톱니바퀴(=cogwheel, gearwheel), 큰 조직 속의 하찮은 일원
a wheel with small bits sticking out around the edge that fit together with the bits of another wheel as they turn in a machine

cohesion
2012 상반기 지방직 9급
화합, 결합, 응집력
a condition in which people or things are closely united

coin
2014 법원사무직 9급
(화폐를) 주조하다, (신어 등을) 만들어 내다, (두뇌를) 이용해 돈을 벌다
to make pieces of money from metal ; to invent a new word or expression, especially one that many people start to use

coincide
2007 행정자치부 9급
(둘 이상의 일이) 동시에 일어나다, (생각·의견 등이) 일치하다, (물건이나 장소가) 만나다
to be the same or similar, to occupy exactly the same space

collapse
2013 제1회 지방직, 2006 중앙선거관리위원회 9급
(건물 등이) 무너지다, 붕괴하다
if a building, wall, etc. collapses, it falls down suddenly, usually because it is weak or damaged

Example Uncle Ted's chair _____ under his weight.

🔲 collapsed

2012 상반기 지방직 9급

colleague

(관직 · 직업상의) 동료(=associate)

someone you work with, used especially by professional people

2005 중앙인사위원회 9급

collide

충돌하다, 부딪치다

to hit something or someone that is moving in a different direction from you ; to disagree strongly with a person or group, especially on a particular subject

2006 서울시 9급

colorful

색채가 풍부한, 다채로운

having bright colors or a lot of different colors

2014 법원사무직 9급

commercial

상업상의, 영리적인, 광고 방송의 ; 광고 방송

related to business and the buying and selling of goods and services ; related to the ability of a product or business to make a profit ; an advertisement on television or radio

Example The film was a huge _____ success.

🔲 commercial

2014 제1차 순경

commit

(죄 · 과실 등을) 범하다, ~을 위임하다, 맡기다

to do something wrong or illegal ; to say that someone will definitely do something or must do something

2013 안전행정부, 2005 중앙인사위원회 9급, 2005 대구시 9급

commitment

공약, 약속, 언질, 책임, 전념, 위탁, 위임

a promise to do something or to behave in a particular way ; the hard work and loyalty that someone gives to an organization, activity, etc. ; something that you have promised you will do or that you have to do

2006 중앙인사위원회 9급

commuter

교외 통근자

someone who travels a long distance to work every day

competition

2014 사회복지직 9급, 2013 제1회 지방직 9급

경쟁, 경기, 시합

a situation in which people or organizations try to be more successful than other people or organizations ; an organized event in which people or teams compete against each other

2005 중앙인사위원회 9급

compile

(자료를 모아) ~을 편찬하다, 편집하다, 만들다

to make a book, list, record, etc., using different pieces of information, music, etc.

2011 행정안전부 9급

complacent

(보통 못마땅함) 현실에 안주하는, 자기만족적인

satisfied with how things are and not wanting to change them

2011 서울시 9급

complicated

복잡한, 뒤얽힌, 풀기 어려운, 이해하기 어려운

difficult to understand or deal with, because many parts or details are involved ; consisting of many closely connected parts

2005 대구시 9급

comprehensible

이해할 수 있는, 알기 쉬운

easy to understand

2006 중앙인사위원회 9급

compromise

타협, 화해, 절충안 ; 타협하다

a situation in which people accept something slightly different from what they really want, because of circumstances or because they are considering the wishes of other people. ; a solution to a problem in which two things or situations are changed slightly so that they can exist together ; If you compromise with someone, you reach an agreement with them in which you both give up something that you originally wanted. You can also say that two people or groups compromise.

2013 안전행정부, 2007 행정자치부 9급

conceive

(생각 · 계획 등을) 마음속으로 하다(품다), 임신하다

to devise in the mind ; imagine, become pregnant with (a child)

2006 서울시 9급

concentration

집중, 몰두

the ability to think about something carefully or for a long time

concern

2014 법원사무직 9급, 2013 서울특별시

~에 관계하다(=relate to), ~에 관계가 있다, ~에 관한 것이다, 걱정시키다 ; 관계, 관심(사), 걱정, 근심

if a story, book, report, etc. concerns someone or something, it is about them ; to make someone feel worried or upset ; if an activity, situation, rule, etc. concerns you, it affects you or involves you ; a feeling of worry about something important

conclusion

2005 국회사무처 8급

결론, 결말

something you decide after considering all the information you have ; the end or final part of something

concrete

2005 대구시 9급

콘크리트 ; 구체적인, 명확한(↔ abstract)

a substance used for building that is made by mixing sand, small stones, cement, and water ; definite and specific

condescending

2012 행정안전부 9급

거들먹거리는, 잘난 체하는

treating someone as if you are better or more important than them

concurrent

2008 행정안전부 9급

공존하는, 동시에 발생하는

happening or existing at the same time

condone

2005 국회사무처 8급

묵인하다, (죄를) 용서하다

to accept or forgive behavior that most people think is morally wrong

conduct

2013 안전행정부 · 서울특별시, 2006 중앙인사위원회 9급

수행하다, 안내하다

to carry out a particular activity or process, especially in order to get information or prove facts ; to take or lead someone somewhere

confessional

2005 대구시 9급

고백의, 자백의, 신앙 고백의

confessional speech or writing contains private thoughts or feelings that you would normally keep secret

conflict

2006 중앙인사위원회 9급

논쟁, 대립, 투쟁

a state of disagreement or argument between people, groups, countries, etc. ; fighting or a war

congested

2005 중앙인사위원회 9급

(사람·교통 등이) 붐비는, 혼잡한, 정체한

full of traffic

> Example London's roads are heavily _____.
>
> 🄴 congested

Congress

2011 서울시 9급, 2005 국회사무처 8급

(미국의) 국회, 의회[상원(the Senate)과 하원(the House of Representatives)의 양원제]

the group of people elected to make laws in the US, consisting of the Senate and the House of Representatives

conservative

2016 지방직 9급

보수적인

A Conservative politician or voter is a member of or votes for the Conservative Party in Britain.

consecutive

2006 중앙인사위원회 9급

연속적인, 계속되는

consecutive numbers or periods of time follow one after the other without any interruptions

consensus

2005 중앙인사위원회 9급

(의견 등의) 일치, 합의, 일치된 의견, 여론

an opinion that everyone in a group agrees with or accepts

considerable

2005 국회사무처 8급

상당한, 중요한

fairly large, especially large enough to have an effect or be important

considered

2013 안전행정부, 2006 서울시 9급

존경받는, 중히 여겨지는

a considered opinion, reply, judgment, etc. is one that you have thought about carefully

consign

2008 하반기 지방직 9급

(무엇을 없애기 위해 어디에) 놓다[두다], (좋지 않은 상황에) 처하게 만들다, ~에게 ~을 보내다

to send something to someone, to put (someone) in a usually unpleasant place or situation, to putsomething in a place where old things are stored orthrown away

consistent	2010 서울시 9급, 2005 대구시 9급
	(의견 등이) 일치하는, 모순되지 않은, (사람이) 언행이 일치하는, 시종일관된 (↔ inconsistent)
	always behaving in the same way or having the same attitudes, standards, etc. — usually used to show approval
constant	2014 사회복지직 9급
	끊임없는, 지속적인, 일정한, 불변의
	happening regularly or all the time ; staying the same
constantly	2005 국회사무처 8급
	끊임없이, 빈번하게
	all the time, or very often

Example He talked _____ about his work.

답 constantly

consume	2013 안전행정부
	소비하다, 다 써 버리다
	to use time, energy, goods, etc.
contemplate	2005 국회사무처 8급
	~을 숙고하다(=consider)
	to think about something that you might do in the future
contemporary	2014 법원사무직 9급, 2005 국회사무처 8급
	같은 시대[시기]의 사람
	someone who lived or was in a particular place at the same time as someone else
content	2014 법원사무직 9급, 2005 국회사무처 8급
	내용(물), 목차 ; 만족하는
	the things that are inside a box, bag, room, etc. ; the things that are written in a letter, book, etc. ; the amount of a substance that is contained in something, especially food or drink ; happy and satisfied
contradict	2011 행정안전부 9급, 2006 중앙선거관리위원회 9급
	(사실 · 진술이) 모순되다, 부정하다, 부인하다
	if one statement, story etc contradicts another, the facts in it are different so that both statements cannot be true ; to disagree with something, especially by saying that the opposite is true

Example The witness statements _____ each other and the facts remain unclear.

🔲 contradict

2013 안전행정부

contrast

대조, 대비, 대조적인 것, 화면의 명암 대비 ; 대조하다, 대비하다

a difference between people, ideas, situations, things, etc. that are being compared ; something that is very different from something else ; the differences in color, or between light and dark, that an artist uses in paintings or photographs to make a particular effect ; if two things contrast, the difference between them is very easy to see and is sometimes surprising ; to compare two things, ideas, people, etc. to show how different they are from each other

2014 제1차 순경

convert

변하게 하다, 전환하다, 개조하다, 개종시키다

to change something into a different form of thing, or to change something so that it can be used for a different purpose or in a different way ; to change into a different form of thing, or change into something that can be used for a different purpose or in a different way ; to persuade someone to change to a different religion

2016 서울특별시 9급

convict

유죄를 선고하다

If someone is convicted of a crime, they are found guilty of that crime in a law court.

2005 국회사무처 8급

corruption

(도덕적) 부패, 타락, (언어의) 순수성 상실, 전와

dishonest, illegal, or immoral behavior, especially from someone with power ; a changed form of something, for example a word

2006 중앙인사위원회 9급

count

중요하다, 세다, 계산하다

to be important or valuable ; to calculate the total number of things or people in a group

2005 국회사무처 8급

countenance

(사람·행동 등에 대해) 호의를 보이다, 찬성하다, 묵인하다, 허용하다

to accept, support, or approve of something

courageous

용기 있는, 용감한, 담력이 있는

brave

Example He was wrong, and _____ enough to admit it.

📄 courageous

courtesy

공손함, 정중함, (격식을 차리는 상황에서) 예의상 하는 말[행동], 무료의

polite behavior or remark, to get something free of charge

cover

취재하다, 뉴스로 보도방송하다

to report the details of an event for a newspaper or a television or radio programme

cowardly

겁 많은, 용기가 없는, 비겁한, 비열한

lacking courage

cranium

(*pl.* crania) 두개, 두개골

the part of your head that is made of bone and covers your brain

creed

(일반적으로) 신념, 신조, 주의, 강령

a set of beliefs or principles

crisis

(*pl.* crises) 위기

a situation in which there are a lot of problems that must be dealt with quickly so that the situation does not get worse or more dangerous

Example The country now faces an economic _____.

📄 crisis

criterion

(*pl.* criteria) 기준, 척도

a standard that you use to judge something or make a decision about something

critical	2013 제1회 지방직, 2005 대구시 9급 비평(가)의, 평론의, 비판적인, 위기의, 결정적인 criticizing if you are critical, you criticize someone or something ; something that is critical is very important because what happens in the future depends on it ; a critical time or situation is serious and worrying because things might suddenly become much worse
cue	2006 중앙선거관리위원회 9급, 2005 국회사무처 8급 ~에게 신호를 주다 ; 신호, 계시, 단서, 암시 to give someone a sign that it is the right moment for them to speak or do something, especially during a performance ; an action or event that is a signal for something else to happen ; a word, phrase, or action in a play that is a signal for the next person to speak or act
curb	2005 국회사무처 8급 억제하다(=restrain, check) to control or limit something in order to prevent it from having a harmful effect
curfew	2014 제1회 지방직 9급, 2009 상반기 지방직 9급 통행금지령, (부모가 자녀에게 부과하는) 귀가 시간 an order or law that requires people to be indoors after a certain time at night, the period of time when such an order or law is in effect
cynic	2005 중앙인사위원회 9급 냉소적인 사람, 비꼬는 사람 someone who is not willing to believe that people have good, honest, or sincere reasons for doing something
damaging	2013 안전행정부, 2006 중앙선거관리위원회 9급 손해를 끼치는, 해로운 causing physical harm to someone or something ; affecting someone or something in a bad way
death sentence	2006 서울시 9급 사형 선고 the official punishment of death, ordered by a judge
define	2014 서울시 9급, 2012 행정안전부 9급 ~을 정의하다, (경계 · 범위를) 한정하다 to describe something correctly and thoroughly, and to say what standards, limits, qualities, etc. it has that make it different from other things

🌐 **Example** The duties of the post are difficult to _____.

📗 define

2008 행정안전부 9급

dejected
실의에 빠진, 낙담한
unhappy, disappointed or without hope

2013 서울특별시, 2006 중앙선거관리위원회 9급

delay
지체, 지연, 연기
when someone or something has to wait, or the length of the waiting time ; when something does not happen or start when it should do

🌐 **Example** They must restore normal services without _____.

📗 delay

2005 중앙인사위원회 9급

deliberate
심사숙고한, 계획적인, 신중한
intended or planned

2016 서울특별시 9급

disparate
비행의, 범죄 성향을 보이는
Someone, usually a young person, who is delinquent repeatedly commits minor crimes.

2009 상반기 지방직 9급

denote
조짐을 보여주다[나타내다], 의미하다
to represent something

2006 중앙인사위원회 9급

density
밀도, 농도
the degree to which an area is filled with people or things

2004 중앙선거관리위원회 9급

deposit
(은행에) 예금하다, (정확하게) ~을 놓다[두다], (자동판매기 등에) (돈을) 넣다 ; 예금(액), 맡김, 보관
to put money or something valuable in a bank or other place where it will be safe ; to put something down in a particular place

depression

2005 국회사무처 8급

의기소침, 우울(증), 불경기, 불황

a medical condition that makes you very unhappy and anxious and often prevents you from living a normal life ; a feeling of sadness that makes you think there is no hope for the future ; a long period during which there is very little business activity and a lot of people do not have jobs

derivative

2012 상반기 지방직 9급

파생어, 파생물, (보통 못마땅함) 다른 것을 본뜬, 새롭지 않은

not the result of new ideas, but has been developed from something else

descent

2006 중앙선거관리위원회 9급

가계, 혈통, 강하(降下), 하강

your family origins, especially your nationality or relationship to someone important who lived a long time ago ; the process of going down

 Example : Passengers must fasten their seat belts prior to _____.

📖 descent

desirable

2011 상반기 지방직 9급, 2006 중앙인사위원회 9급

바람직한, 매력 있는

something that is desirable is worth having or doing ; sexually attractive

desirability

2011 상반기 지방직 9급

바람직한, 바람직한 상황

wished for as being attractive, useful, or necessary

desolate

2007 행정자치부 9급

황량한, 적막한, (장소가) 너무나 외로운

a place that is empty and not attractive, with no people or nothing pleasant in it

despite

2015 인사혁신처 9급

~에도 불구하고(=in spite of)

used to say that something happens or is true even though something else might have prevented it

_____ all our efforts to save the school, the authorities decided to close it.

🔑 Despite

2011 행정안전부 9급

detective
탐정, 형사 ; 탐정의, 탐지용의
a police officer whose job is to discover information about crimes and catch criminals

2015 사회복지직 9급, 2005 대구시 9급

deter
(공포·의혹 등으로) ~을 그만두게[단념하게] 하다
to stop someone from doing something, by making them realize it will be difficult or have bad results

2015 사회복지직 9급

device
장치, 고안(물), 계획, 방책, 책략
a machine or tool that does a special job

2011 행정안전부 9급

dexterity
(손이나 머리를 쓰는) 재주
skill in performing tasks, especially with the hands or brain

2006 중앙선거관리위원회 9급

dictate
지령하다, 지시하다, 구술하다
to tell someone exactly what they must do or how they must behave ; to say words for someone else to write down

2007 국회사무처 9급, 2005 국회사무처 8급

dignity
존엄, 품위, (말씨·태도 등의) 엄숙함, 명예
the ability to behave in a calm controlled way even in a difficult situation

2005 국회사무처 8급

directness
똑바름, 직접적임, 솔직함
the quality of being clear, plain, or easy to understand

2010 상반기 지방직 9급

discharged
(어떤 장소나 직무에서) 해고하다, 석방하다, (기체·액체·에너지가) 방출되다, (임무 등을) 이행하다, 발사 하다
officially allow someone to leave somewhere, to emit or send out a liquid, gas, or other substance, to do all that is required to fulfill

disciplined

2012 하반기 지방직 9급, 2009 상반기 지방직 9급

훈련 받은, 잘 통솔된

behaving in a very controlled way

discourage

2009 상반기 지방직 9급

~의 용기를 잃게 하다, 낙담시키다, 단념시키다

to make someone less confident or less willing to do something ; to persuade someone not to do something, especially by making it seem difficult or bad

discouraged

2005 대구시 9급

낙담한, 낙심한

no longer having the confidence you need to continue doing something

discriminate

2015 사회복지직 9급

구별하다, 차별하다, 차별 대우하다

to recognize a difference between things ; to treat a person or group differently from another in an unfair way

disdain

2015 사회복지직 9급

경멸, 모멸, 거만한 태도(of) ; ~을 경멸하다

a complete lack of respect that you show for someone or something because you think they are not important or good enough ; to have no respect for someone or something, because you think they are not important or good enough

disinformation

2005 국회사무처 8급

(고의적인) 오보, 허위 정보

false information which is given deliberately in order to hide the truth or confuse people, especially in political situations

dispute

2006 중앙인사위원회 9급

논쟁, 분쟁 ; 논쟁하다, 토의하다

a serious argument or disagreement ; to argue or disagree with someone

---

Example The firm is involved in a legal _____ with a rival company.

답 dispute

---

disparate	이질적인, 다른 2016 지방직 9급 Disparate things are clearly different from each other in quality or type.
disrespect	무례, 결례 2011 상반기 지방직 9급 speech or behavior which shows that you do not think someone or something
distinction	구별, 차별, 차이, 특징 2013 제1회 지방직 a clear difference or separation between two similar things
distract	(마음·주의 등을) 딴 데로 돌리다, (정신을) 혼란시키다, 기분 전환을 하다 2010 행정안전부 9급 to take someone's attention away from something by making them look at or listen to something else
distraction	정신 산란, 주의 산만, 심란 2006 서울시 9급, 2005 대구시 9급 something that stops you paying attention to what you are doing
distrust	불신, 의혹 ; 믿지 않다, 의심하다 2014 법원사무직 9급 a feeling that you cannot trust someone ; to not trust someone or something
diversify	(특히 사업체나 회사가 사업을) 다각[다양]화하다, 다양해지다 2013 안전행정부, 2010 상반기 지방직 9급 to become more varied or different
diversity	다양성 2014 제1차 순경, 2006 서울시 9급 the fact of including many different types of people or things ; a range of different people, things, or ideas
divert	방향을 바꾸게 하다[전환시키다], 우회시키다 2014 법원사무직 9급 To divert vehicles or travellers means to make them follow a different route or go to a different destination than they originally intended. You can also say that someone or something diverts from a particular route or to a particular place.

doggedly	2011 행정안전부 9급 억세게 in a way that is stubbornly persistent
doleful	2006 중앙선거관리위원회 9급 서글픈, 슬픈, 슬픔에 잠긴 very sad
dominate	2010 행정안전부 9급 ~을 지배하다, 좌우하다, ~보다 우세하다 to control someone or something or to have more importance than other people or things
doom	2005 국회사무처 8급 ~을 운명짓다, ~의 운명을 정하다 ; (좋지 않은) 운명 to make someone or something certain to fail, die, be destroyed, etc. ; something very bad that is going to happen, or the fact that it is going to happen
doorknob	2014 법원사무직 9급, 2011 행정안전부 9급 (문의) 손잡이 a round handle that you turn to open a door
dose	2011 기상청 9급 (약의) 1회 복용량, 쓴 약 ; ~을 복용시키다, 약을 먹다 the amount of a medicine or a drug that you should take ; to give someone medicine or a drug
double-check	2005 중앙인사위원회 9급 재확인하다 ; 재확인 to check something again so that you are completely sure it is correct, safe, etc.
double-digit	2010 상반기 지방직 9급 (인플레이션 · 실업률 등이) 두 자리 수의 relating to a number or series of numbers between 10 and 99:
drain	2013 서울시 9급 (액체를) 서서히 배출하다, (도시 · 집 등에) 배수 설비를 하다, (재산 등을) 써서 없애다 to make the water or liquid in something flow away ; to use too much of something, especially money, so that there is not enough left

drama

2014 법원사무직 9급

대본, 극, 희곡, 연극

acting — used when talking about it as a subject to study or teach ; a play for the theater, television, radio, etc., usually a serious one, or plays in general

dramatic

2014 법원사무직 9급, 2005 국회사무처 8급

극적인, 희곡의

great and sudden ; exciting or impressive ; connected with acting or plays

drop

2013 제1회 지방직, 2005 중앙인사위원회 9급

(습관 등을) 그만두다, (의논 등을) 중단하다

to stop doing something, discussing something, or continuing with something

Example The proposal was _____ after opposition from civil liberties groups.

📝 dropped

dull

2014 법원사무직 9급

따분한, 재미없는

If you describe someone or something as dull, you mean they are not interesting or exciting.

duplicate

2009 행정안전부 9급

복제(물), 사본, 복사 ; 이중의, 중복의, 복사한

an exact copy of something that you can use in the same way ; exactly the same as something, or made as an exact copy of something

dwell

2013 국회사무처 9급

거주하다, 살다

to live in a particular place

economic

2015 인사혁신처 9급, 2014 사회복지직 9급, 2013 안전행정부, 2005 대구시 9급

경제학의, 경제(상)의

relating to trade, industry, and the management of money

effect

2014 사회복지직 9급, 2013 안전행정부, 2005 중앙인사위원회 9급

결과, 영향, 효과 ; (변화 등을) 초래하다, (목적 · 계획 등을) 이루다, 달성하다

the way in which an event, action, or person changes someone or something ; to make something happen

effective	2014 사회복지직 9급, 2013 안전행정부
	유효한, 효력이 있는
	successful, and working in the way that was intended
efficient	2014 사회복지직 9급, 2013 제1회 지방직, 2006 중앙인사위원회 9급
	유능한, 실력 있는
	if someone or something is efficient, they work well without wasting time, money, or energy
elaborate	2008 행정안전부 9급
	애써 만들다, 정교하게 만들다 ; 정교한, 복잡한, 공들인
	to give more details or new information about something ; having a lot of small parts or details put together in a complicated way ; carefully planned and organized in great detail
elastic	2005 중앙인사위원회 9급
	탄성이 있는, 탄성체의
	made of elastic ; a material that is elastic can stretch and then go back to its usual length or size
election	2014 사회복지직 9급
	선거, 표결, 투표
	when people vote to choose someone for an official position
electrocution	2006 서울시 9급
	전기 사형, 감전사
	execution by electricity
elemental	2006 중앙인사위원회 9급
	기본적인, 본질적인, 요소의
	simple, basic, and important
elongate	2016 인사혁신처 9급
	길게 늘이다, 길어지다
	If you elongate something or if it elongates, you stretch it so that it becomes longer.
eliminate	2014 사회복지직 9급, 2012 상반기 지방직 9급, 2006 중앙인사위원회 9급
	~을 제거하다, 삭제하다, 무시하다, 탈락시키다
	to completely get rid of something that is unnecessary or unwanted ; to defeat a team or person in a competition, so that they no longer take part in it

	2006 중앙선거관리위원회 9급
elite	엘리트(층), 최상류층 사람들
	a group of people who have a lot of power and influence because they have money, knowledge, or special skills
	2009 행정안전부 9급
emancipate	(법적·정치적·사회적 제약에서) 해방시키다
	set free, especially from legal, social, or political restrictions
	2005 국회사무처 8급
embody	구체화하다, 구현하다
	to be a very good example of an idea or quality
	2011 상반기 지방직 9급
embossed	양각으로 무늬를 넣은, 돋을새김의
	to decorate an object, especially with letters, using special tools which make a raised mark on its surface
	2006 중앙선거관리위원회 9급
emerge	나오다, 나타나다(=appear)
	to appear or come out from somewhere
	2006 중앙인사위원회 9급
emergency room	응급실
	a part of a hospital that immediately helps people who have been hurt in an accident or who are extremely ill
	2005 중앙인사위원회 9급
emission	(빛·열·향기 등의) 방사, 발산, 방사[배출]물
	a gas or other substance that is sent into the air ; the act of sending out light, heat, gas, etc.
	2014 법원사무직 9급
emphasis	강조, 역점, 주안점
	Emphasis is special or extra importance that is given to an activity or to a part or aspect of something
	2006 중앙선거관리위원회 9급
empire	제국
	a group of countries that are all controlled by one ruler or government
	2009 행정안전부 9급
emulate	(흠모하는 대상을) 모방하다[따라 가다], (컴퓨터 프로그램 등이) 모방하다
	to try to be likesomeone or something you admire

encroach

2016 서울특별시 9급

침해하다, 잠식하다

If one thing encroaches on another, the first thing spreads or becomes stronger, and slowly begins to restrict the power, range, or effectiveness of the second thing.

encounter

2011 법원행정처 9급

(우연히) 만나다, 마주치다, (곤란 · 반대 등에) 부닥치다, (토론 등에서 상대편과) 대립하다 ; 마주침, 조우, (의견의) 대립, 충돌

to meet someone without planning to ; to experience something, especially problems or opposition ; an occasion when you meet someone, or do something with someone you do not know

endanger

2006 중앙인사위원회 9급

위태롭게 하다, 위험에 빠뜨리다

to put someone or something in danger of being hurt, damaged, or destroyed

enhance

2014 제1회 지방직 9급, 2013 안전행정부

향상하다, (가치 · 능력 · 매력 등을) 높이다, 늘리다

to improve something

Example   The publicity has _____ his reputation.

🔲 enhanced

---

enlive

2006 중앙인사위원회 9급

활기차게 만들다, 유쾌하게 하다

to make something more interesting

entail

2013 서울시 9급

(필연적인 결과로서) ~을 일으키다, 수반하다, (비용 · 노력 등을) 필요로 하다

to involve something as a necessary part or result

enterprise

2013 서울시 9급

기획, 모험적인 계획, 기업, 사업

a company, organization, or business ; a large and complicated project, especially one that is done with a group of other people

enthusiasm

2012 행정안전부 9급

열중, 열광, 열의

a strong feeling of interest and enjoyment about something and an eagerness to be involved in it

envy	2013 서울시 9급
	부러워하다, 시기하다, 질투하다 ; 질투, 선망, 시기
	to wish that you had someone else's possessions, abilities, etc. ; the feeling of wanting something that someone else has
erupt	2012 상반기 지방직 9급
	(화산 등이) 폭발하다, (감정이) 폭발하다, (전쟁이) 발발하다
	if a volcano erupts, it explodes and sends smoke, fire, and rock into the sky ; if fighting, violence, noise, etc. erupts, it starts suddenly ; if a place or situation erupts, there is a sudden increase in activity or emotion
escalate	2012 상반기 지방직 9급
	확대[증가, 악화] 되다.
	to make or become greater or more serious
estimate	2013 제1회 지방직, 2006 중앙인사위원회 9급
	어림잡다 ; 추정치
	to try to judge the value, size, speed, cost, etc. of something, without calculating it exactly ; a calculation of the value, size, amount, etc. of something
eternal	2005 대구시 9급
	영원한, 끊임없는, 불변의
	continuing forever and having no end ; seeming to continue forever, especially because of being boring or annoying
euthanasia	2010 행정안전부 9급
	안락사, 안락사술
	the deliberate killing of a person who is very ill and going to die, in order to stop them suffering
euphemism	2011 행정안전부 9급
	완곡 어구[표현]
	a word or phrase used to avoid saying an unpleasant or offensive word
eventually	2014 법원사무직 · 안전행정부 9급, 2013 안전행정부, 2005 대구시 9급
	최후에는, 마침내, 결국(=finally, ultimately, after all, in the end, in the long run, in conclusion)
	after a long time, or after a lot of things have happened
evidence	2013 안전행정부, 2006 서울시 9급
	증거, 흔적
	facts or signs that show clearly that something exists or is true

evolution	2006 중앙선거관리위원회 9급 전개, (사건 등의) 발전, (종(種)·기관 등의) 진화(론), (가스·열 등의) 방출 the scientific idea that plants and animals develop and change gradually over a long period of time ; the gradual change and development of an idea, situation, or object
evolve	2013 안전행정부, 2006 중앙선거관리위원회 9급 진화하다, (이론·의견 등을) 전개하다, 발전시키다, (결론·법칙 등을) 이끌어 내다, 도출하다 if an animal or plant evolves, it changes gradually over a long period of time ; to develop and change gradually over a long period of time
exceed	2013 안전행정부 ~보다 크다, ~을 능가하다, (범위·한도를) 넘어서다, (양이나 정도 등을) 초과하다 to be more than a particular number or amount ; to go beyond what rules or laws say you are allowed to do
excessive	2014 법원사무직 9급, 2011 행정안전부 9급 과도한, 터무니없는, 극단적인 much more than is reasonable or necessary
exchange	2014 법원사무직 9급 교환, 교역, 언쟁, 논쟁 the act of giving someone something and receiving something else from them ; a short conversation, usually between two people who are angry with each other
exclusive	2013 제1회 지방직, 2006 서울시 9급 배타[배제]적인, 독점적인 available or belonging only to particular people, and not shared
excusable	2010 상반기 지방직 9급 변명(용서 / 용납)이 되는 deserving to be forgiven
exhilarating	2008 하반기 지방직 9급 아주 신나는 [즐거운] making you feel very excited and happy
existing	2005 중앙인사위원회 9급 현존하는, 존재하는, 현행의, 지금의 present or being used now

expectation

2010 행정안전부 9급, 2005 중앙인사위원회 9급

기대, 예상

what you think or hope will happen ; a feeling or belief about the way something should be or how someone should behave

experiment

2011 서울시 9급

~로 실험하다, 시험하다(in, on, with) ; (연구 · 과학상의) 실험, 시험

to try using various ideas, methods, etc. to find out how good or effective they are ; to do a scientific test to find out if a particular idea is true or to obtain more information ; a process in which you test a new idea or method to see if it is useful or effective

expiable

2012 상반기 지방직 9급

보상할 수 있는

capable of being expiated or atoned for

explicable

2012 상반기 지방직 9급

설명[해명]되는

able to be explained

explode

2013 안전행정부

폭발시키다, 파열시키다, 타파하다

to burst, or to make something burst, into small pieces, usually with a loud noise and in a way that causes damage

explosion

2013 안전행정부 9급

폭발 ; 폭파

An explosion is a sudden, violent burst of energy, for example one caused by a bomb.

expressive

2005 국회사무처 8급

표현이 풍부한, (감정 등을) 나타내는, 표현적인

showing very clearly what someone thinks or feels

exquisite

2008 상반기 지방직 9급

매우 아름다운, 정교한, 강렬한, 예민한

very beautiful and delicate, intensely felt

extended

2005 국회사무처 8급

연장된, 장기화된

made longer or bigger ; long or longer than expected or planned

extensive

2014 안전행정부 9급

광대한, 넓은, 대규모의

large in size, amount, or degree

Example Fire has caused _____ damage to the island's forests.

📖 extensive

extract

2013 안전행정부

~을 뽑다, (원리 · 해석 등을) 끌어내다, 추론하다

to remove an object from somewhere, especially with difficulty ; to carefully remove a substance from something which contains it, using a machine, chemical process, etc.

extravagant

2012 하반기 지방직 9급

낭비하는, 사치스러운, 엄청난, 터무니없는

spending or costing a lot of money, especially more than is necessary or more than you can afford

facial

2013 안전행정부, 2005 국회사무처 8급

얼굴의, 안면의

on your face or relating to your face

factionalism

2005 국회사무처 8급

당파심, 당파 근성, 파벌 싸움, 파벌주의

disagreements between different groups within an organization

fair

2013 안전행정부

(대규모의) 박람회, 바자회

an outdoor event, at which there are large machines to ride on, games to play, and sometimes farm animals being judged and sold ; an event at which people or businesses show and sell their products

falter

2016 인사혁신처 9급

비틀거리다, 불안정해지다, 흔들리다

If something falters, it loses power or strength in an uneven way, or no longer makes much progress.

familiar

2011 법원행정처 9급, 2006 중앙인사위원회 9급

잘 알고 있는

someone or something that is familiar is well-known to you and easy to recognize

fantasize	2008 하반기 지방직 9급 공상하다, 환상을 갖다 to imagine things only possible in fantasy
far-sighted	2005 중앙인사위원회 9급 선견지명이 있는, 현명한 far-sighted people, ideas, or plans are wise because they show an understanding of what will happen in the future
fart	2010 행정안전부 9급 (특히 소리가 크게 나게) 방귀를 뀌다 to release gas from the anus
fasting	2013 제1회 지방직 단식, 금식, 절식 the Muslim holy month of fasting and prayer.
fateful	2010 서울시 9급, 2001 법원서기보 숙명적인, 운명적인, 결정적인 having an important, especially bad, effect on future events
fatigue	2014 법원사무처 9급 피로, 피곤, 노고 ; ~을 지치게 하다 very great tiredness
favorable	2006 서울시 9급 호의적인, 유리한 a favorable report, opinion, or reaction shows that you think that someone or something is good or that you agree with them
fearlessly	2006 중앙선거관리위원회 9급 겁 없이, 대담무쌍하게 without fear
fearlessness	2006 중앙선거관리위원회 9급 겁 없음, 대담무쌍 feeling no fear
feasible	2010 상반기 지방직 9급 실행할 수 있는, 실현 가능한, 그럴듯한, 있음직한 a plan, idea, or method that is feasible is possible and is likely to work

feasibility	2010 상반기 지방직 9급 실행할 수 있음, (실행) 가능성	whether something can be made, done or achieved, or is reasonable
feature	2013 안전행정부 ~을 특집 기사로 다루다, 대서특필하다, ~의 특징을 이루다	to include or show something as a special or important part of something, or to be included as an important part
feed	2014 안전행정부 9급 ~에게 먹을 것을 주다, 먹이다, ~을 기르다, 사육하다	to give food to a person or animal ; to give a special substance to a plant, which helps it grow
feudal	2006 중앙선거관리위원회 9급 봉건(제도)의, 봉건적인, 중세(Middle Ages)의	relating to feudalism
fictionalize	2012 행정안전부 9급 (실화를) 소설화[영화화]하다	to write about a real event or character, but adding imaginary details and changing the real facts
financier	2005 대구시 9급 재정가, 금융업자, 자본가	someone who controls or lends large sums of money
fiscal	2005 국회사무처 8급 국고의, 국가 세입의, 재정상의, 회계의	relating to money, taxes, debts, etc. that are owned and managed by the government
flaw	2016 서울특별시 9급 (사물의) 결함	A flaw in something such as a theory or argument is a mistake in it, which causes it to be less effective or valid.
fling	2005 대구시 9급 ~을 던지다, 내던지다	to throw something somewhere using a lot of force
flourish	2014 안전행정부 9급, 2006 중앙인사위원회 9급 번영하다, 융성하다, (칼·팔 등을) (위협적으로) 휘두르다 ; (칼 등의) 휘두르기, 과시, 융성, 번영	to develop well and be successful ; to wave something in your hand in order to make people notice it

flowing	2006 중앙선거관리위원회 9급

flowing

풍성하게 늘어진, 흐르는

hanging or moving in a smooth graceful way ; continuing in a smooth, graceful way, with no sudden changes

2014 서울시 9급

flu

인플루엔자, 유행성 감기, 독감(=influenza)

a common illness that makes you feel very tired and weak, gives you a sore throat, and makes you cough and have to clear your nose a lot

2006 서울시 9급

forgive

용서하다

to stop being angry with someone and stop blaming them, although they have done something wrong

2005 국회사무처 8급

formality

형식적임, 형식에 구애됨, 정식 절차

something that you must do as a formal or official part of an activity or process

2010 행정안전부 9급

formula

처리 방안, 방식, 공식, 상투적인 문구, 판에 박힌 말

a method or set of principles that you use to solve a problem or to make sure that something is successful ; a fixed and familiar series of words that seems meaningless or insincere

2005 국회사무처 8급

fortify

~을 강화하다, 기운을 북돋우다, 요새화하다

to encourage an attitude or feeling and make it stronger ; to build towers, walls, etc. around an area or city in order to defend it

2005 중앙인사위원회 9급, 2005 국회사무처 8급

fragile

깨지기 쉬운, 망가지기 쉬운, (체질이) 허약한

easily broken or damaged ; a weak physical condition because of illness

2006 중앙선거관리위원회 9급

fragmented

파편이 된, 분열한

broken into small fragments

2008 상반기 지방직 9급

frantic

정신 없이[미친 듯이] 서두르는, (두려움 · 걱정으로) 제정신이 아닌

almost out of control because of extreme emotion, such as worry

fratricide	2006 중앙인사위원회 9급 형제 살해, 동포 살해 the crime of murdering your brother or sisterskill
fraud	2009 행정안전부 9급 기만, 사기, 사기 행위, 사기꾼 the crime of deceiving people in order to gain something such as money or goods ; someone or something that is not what it is claimed to be
friendly	2013 서울특별시, 2006 서울시 9급 친한, 친절한, 호의적인 behaving towards someone in a way that shows you like them and are ready to talk to them or help them
frigid	2011 행정안전부 9급 몹시 추운[찬], 냉랭한, (여자가) 불감증의 very cold, chilly in manner, sexually unresponsive, especially of a woman
frugality	2010 상반기 지방직 9급 절약, 검소 sparing or economical as regards money or food
frustration	2012 행정안전부 9급, 2005 대구시 9급 좌절(감), 실패, 낙담, 욕구 불만 the feeling of being annoyed, upset, or impatient, because you cannot control or change a situation, or achieve something ; the fact of being prevented from achieving what you are trying to achieve
fulfill	2009 행정안전부 9급 (의무 · 직무 등을) 완수하다, (약속을) 이행하다, (요구 · 조건 등을) 만족시키다 if you fulfill a hope, wish, or aim, you achieve the thing that you hoped for, wished for, etc.
futile	2016 인사혁신처 9급 쓸데없는, 헛된, 소용없는 If you say that something is futile, you mean there is no point in doing it, usually because it has no chance of succeeding.
galvanometer	2008 하반기 지방직 9급 검류계(檢流計) a device used to indicate the presence and direction of a small electric current

	2005 대구시 9급
gem	보석
	a beautiful stone that has been cut into a special shape
	2013 제1회 지방직
gene	유전자, 유전 인자
	a part of a cell in a living thing that controls what it looks like, how it grows, and how it develops. People get their genes from their parents
	2006 서울시 9급
generous	관대한
	someone who is generous is willing to give money, spend time, etc., in order to help people or give them pleasure
	2008 하반기 지방직 9급, 2006 중앙인사위원회 9급
genocide	(민족 전체를 말살하려는) 대량 학살
	the deliberate murder of a whole group or race of people
	2014 법원사무직 9급, 2006 중앙선거관리위원회 9급
gift	재능, 선물
	a natural ability ; something that you give someone, for example to thank them or because you like them, especially on a special occasion
	2013 안전행정부, 2005 대구시 9급
given	~을 가정하면, ~이 주어지면
	taking something into account
	2008 상반기 지방직 9급
glob	(액체의) 작은 방울, 덩어리, 반고체의 구슬
	a round mass of a thick liquid or a sticky substance
	2007 행정자치부 9급
goof-up	(특히 부주의 · 태만으로)실수를 저지르는 사람, 실수, 고장
	a person who avoids work or responsibility, to avoid doing any work
	2013 안전행정부
Gov., gov.	government(정치, 정부), governor(통치자)
	the written abbreviation of governor
	2014 제1회 지방직 9급, 2006 중앙선거관리위원회 9급
gradual	점차적인, 점진적인
	happening slowly over a long period of time

graduate	2011 상반기 지방직 9급, 2006 서울시 9급
	~에게 학위를 수여하다, ~을 졸업시키다, 졸업하다 ; 졸업생
	to obtain a degree, especially a first degree, from a college or university ; to give a degree or diploma to someone who has completed a course
grasp	2007 중앙인사위원회
	붙잡다, 움켜쥐다
	to take and hold something firmly
grating	2008 하반기 지방직 9급
	(창문·하수구 등의) 쇠창살소리·목소리가 귀에 거슬리는, 삐걱거리는
	to describe a sound which is unpleasant and annoying
grit	2008 상반기 지방직 9급
	모래, 투지, 빙판에 모래[소금 등]를 뿌리다
	small loose particles of stone or sand, spread grit on (an icy road)
groundwater	2005 중앙인사위원회 9급
	지하수
	water that is below the ground
grudge	2006 서울시 9급
	원한, 악의, 불만
	a feeling of dislike for someone because you cannot forget that they harmed you in the past
guilt-ridden	2012 행정안전부 9급
	죄책감
	feeling very guilty
gullible	2006 서울시 9급
	잘 속는(=credulous, easily deceived)
	too ready to believe what other people tell you, so that you are easily tricked
hallway	2008 상반기 지방직 9급
	복도, 통로
	a corridor in a building that connects rooms
handicapped	2008 행정안전부 9급
	신체[정신]적 장애가 있는, 핸디캡이 있는 ; 신체[정신] 장애자
	if someone is handicapped, a part of their body or their mind has been permanently injured or damaged. Some people think that this word is offensive ; people who are handicapped. Some people think that this expression is offensive

handling	2011 법원행정처 9급
	취급, 처리, 솜씨, (상품의) 출하
	the way in which someone does a job or deals with a situation, problem, or person
harbor	2006 서울시 9급
	(계획·생각 등을) 품다
	to keep bad thoughts, fears, or hopes in your mind for a long time
harmful	2013 제1회 지방직, 2006 서울시 9급
	유해한, 해로운
	causing or likely to cause harm
hassle	2009 상반기 지방직 9급
	귀찮은[번거로운] 상황[일], 귀찮을 정도로 따지기
	irritating inconvenience
heartbeat	2006 중앙선거관리위원회 9급
	심장 박동
	the action or sound of your heart as it pumps blood through your body
heated	2013 안전행정부 9급, 2006 서울시 9급
	격한, 흥분한, 뜨거워진, 가열된
	an argument, etc. that is full of angry and excited feelings ; a heated swimming pool, room, etc. is made warm using a heater
hectic	2009 상반기 지방직 9급
	정신 없이 바쁜, 빡빡한
	very busy and filled with activity
hermaphroditically	2012 상반기 지방직 9급
	남녀추니의, 암수 한 몸의; 상반된 두 성질을 가진
	a person, plant, or animal that has both male and female parts
hiccup	2008 서울시 9급
	딸꾹질 ; 딸꾹질하다, 딸꾹질하면서 말하다
	a sudden repeated stopping of the breath, usually caused by eating or drinking too fast ; to have hiccups
high-placed	2009 상반기 지방직 9급
	(산꼭대기의) 신전, 제단, 예배소, 중요한 직위, 고관
	in high places, set a high value on, someone in high places

hoarder	2008 하반기 지방직 9급
	축적가
	a store of money or valued objects
homicide	2006 중앙인사위원회 9급
	살인(죄), 살인 행위
	the crime of murder
hookup	2006 중앙선거관리위원회 9급
	접속, 중계, 연결
	a device providing a connection between a power source and a user
hopeful	2005 대구시 9급
	희망에 찬, 기대하고 있는, 전도유망한
	believing that what you hope for is likely to happen ; making you feel that what you hope for is likely to happen
horrible	2005 대구시 9급
	무서운, 끔찍한, 소름끼치는(=hideous)
	very bad — used for example about things you see, taste, or smell, or about the weather ; very unpleasant and often frightening, worrying, or upsetting
horseback riding	2006 중앙선거관리위원회 9급
	승마
	riding a horse as a sport
hospitable	2006 서울시 9급
	환대하는, 대접이 좋은
	friendly, welcoming, and generous to visitors
hostile	2006 서울시 9급
	적(국)의, 적의가 있는, (~에) 반대하는, 적대적인
	belonging to an enemy ; angry and deliberately unfriendly towards someone and ready to argue with them
hostility	2008 서울시 9급
	적의, 적개심, 반항, 전쟁 (상태)
	when someone is unfriendly and full of anger towards another person ; strong or angry opposition to something ; fighting in a war
hound	2009 상반기 지방직 9급
	따라다니며 괴롭히다, 사냥개
	a dog used for hunting, especially a foxhound, to persistently harass

hovered

2009 상반기 지방직 9급

(허공/수줍거나 자신감 없는 태도로 특히 다른 사람 주위를/무엇의 가까이 · 불확실한 상태에) 맴돌다, 서성이다

to stay in one place in the air, usually by moving the wings quickly, stand somewhere, especially near another person, eagerly or nervously waiting for their attention

humanity

2005 국회사무처 8급, 2005 대구시 9급

인류, 인간, 인간성, 자비

people in general ; kindness, respect, and sympathy towards others

humorous

2005 대구시 9급

유머가 넘치는, 해학적인, 익살맞은

funny and enjoyable

hunger

2013 안전행정부, 2012 행정안전부 9급

갈망, 열망

a strong need or desire for something

hydrogen

2005 국회사무처 8급

수소

a colorless gas that is the lightest of all gases, forms water when it combines with oxygen, and is used to produce ammonia and other chemicals. It is a chemical element: symbol H

hyperactive

2008 상반기 지방직 9급

(특히 아동들이나 그들의 행동이) 활동 과잉의

abnormally or extremely active

hypnoid

2010 행정안전부 9급

최면 양(催眠 樣)의, 최면모양의

psychological in a state like or similar to sleep or hypnosis

iceberg

2006 중앙인사위원회 9급

빙산

a very large mass of ice floating in the sea, most of which is under the surface of the water

idealism

2005 대구시 9급

이상주의, 관념론, 관념주의

the belief that you should live your life according to high standards and principles, even when they are very difficult to achieve ; a way of using art or literature to show the world as a perfect place, even though it is not

identify

2013 안전행정부

확인하다, ~이라고 인정하다, 동일시하다

to recognize and correctly name someone or something ; to recognize something or discover exactly what it is, what its nature or origin is, etc.

idiomatic

2006 서울시 9급

관용적인

typical of the natural way in which someone speaks or writes when they are using their own language

ignition

2008 하반기 지방직 9급

점화, 발화, (엔진 등의) 점화 장치

the electrical part of a vehicle's engine that makes it start working ; the place in a car where you put in a key to start the engine ; the act of starting to burn or of making something start to burn

ignore

2013 국회사무처 9급

무시하다, 모르는 체하다

to deliberately pay no attention to something that you have been told or that you know about ; to behave as if you had not heard or seen someone or something

---

 You can't _____ the fact that many criminals never go to prison.

🔲 ignore

---

illegible

2009 행정안전부 9급

읽기 어려운, 판독이 불가능한

not clear enough to be read

illicit

2012 상반기 지방직 9급

불법의, 사회 통념에 어긋나는

illegal or disapproved of by society

illustrate

2014 사회복지직 9급

설명하다, 예증하다, (책 등에) 삽화를 넣다

to make the meaning of something clearer by giving examples ; to be an example which shows that something is true or that a fact exists ; to put pictures in a book, article, etc.

imagination

2014 안전행정부 9급

상상(력), 몽상, 창조력, 창의력

the ability to form pictures or ideas in your mind

impairment	2010 행정안전부 9급
	(신체적 · 정신적) 장애
	a condition in which a part of your body or mind is damaged and does not work well
impart	2008 행정안전부 9급
	(정보 · 지식 등을) 전하다, (특정한 특성을) 주다
	to communicate information to someone, to give something a particular feeling, quality or taste
impede	2016 인사혁신처 9급
	방해하다, 지연시키다, 저해하다
	If you impede someone or something, you make their movement, development, or progress difficult.
imperceptible	2016 서울특별시 9급
	감지할 수 없는
	Something that is imperceptible is so small that it is not noticed or cannot be seen.
implement	2006 중앙인사위원회 9급
	수단, 방법, 도구 ; 이행하다, 수행하다
	a tool, especially one used for outdoor physical work ; to take action or make changes that you have officially decided should happen
implicit	2005 대구시 9급
	함축적인, 암시적인, 맹목적인, 절대적인
	suggested or understood without being stated directly ; forming a central part of something, but without being openly stated ; complete and containing no doubts
imply	2014 안전행정부 9급, 2006 중앙선거관리위원회 9급
	암시하다, 의미하다, 포함하다
	to suggest that something is true, without saying this directly
impractical	2011 행정안전부 9급
	(생각 · 계획 등이) 비실용적인, 비현실적인, (사람 등이) 실천력이 없는 ; 실제로 쓸 수 없는 소도구
	not sensible or possible for practical reasons ; not good at dealing with ordinary practical matters, such as making or repairing things
impressive	2013 제1회 지방직 9급, 2005 대구시 9급
	인상에 남는, 인상적인, 감동적인, 장엄한
	something that is impressive makes you admire it because it is very good, large, important, etc.

imprison	2008 상반기 지방직 9급 교도소[감옥]에 넣다, 수감하다, 가두다, 구속하다 to put someone in prison or to keep them somewhere and prevent them from leaving ; if a situation or feeling imprisons people, it restricts what they can do
imprisonment	2005 대구시 9급 투옥, 구금, 감금, 강제적 속박 the state of being in prison, or the time someone spends there
impulse	2014 안전행정부 9급 추진[력], 충격, 자극, (마음의) 충동 a sudden strong desire to do something without thinking about whether it is a sensible thing to do ; a reason or aim that causes a particular kind of activity or behavior
inadequate	2014 사회복지직 9급 부적당한, 부적절한, 불충분한, 무력한 not good enough, big enough, skilled enough, etc. for a particular purpose ; someone who feels inadequate thinks other people are better, more skillful, more intelligent, etc. than they are
inaugural	2010 상반기 지방직 9급 (공식적인 연설·모임 등에 대해) 취임(식)의, 개회의, 첫 marking the beginning of an institution, activity, or period of office
inauguration	2010 상반기 지방직 9급 대통령·교수 등의) 취임(식), (신시대 등의) 개시, (공공시설 등의) 정식 개업, 준공식, (공공시설 등의) 정식 개시, 개업, 창업, 취임(식) to put someone into an official position with a ceremony, to put something into use or action officially, to mark the beginning of a new period, style or activity
incident	2014 안전행정부 9급, 2004 서울시 9급 사건, 사변, 분쟁 an event, especially one that is unusual, important, or violent ; a serious disagreement between two countries
inconceivable	2008 상반기 지방직 9급 상상[생각]도 할 수 없는 impossible to imagine or think of
inconclusive	2011 행정안전부 9급, 2007 행정자치부 9급 (확고한 결정·결과에 이를 정도로) 결정적이 아닌, 결론에 이르지 못하는 not showing that something is certainly true

		2006 서울시 9급

incongruous ▫ 어울리지 않는, 모순된

strange, unexpected, or unsuitable in a particular situation

2009 상반기 지방직 9급

inconsistencies ▫ 불일치, 모순

not compatible or in keeping with,

incorporate ▫ (일부로) 포함하다, (법인체를) 설립[창립]하다

to take in or include as part of a whole, constitute (a company, city, or other organization) as a legal corporation

increasingly ▫ 점점 더, 더욱더

more and more all the time

indisputable ▫ 반론의 여지가 없는, 부인할 수 없는

impossible to question or doubt

induce ▫ 설득하다, 유도하다, 초래하다

to persuade someone to do something, to cause something to happen or exist

indulge ▫ (특히 좋지 않다고 여겨지는 것을) 마음껏 하다, (특정한 욕구·관심 등을) 충족시키다, ~가 제멋대로 굴게 하다, (특히 불법적인 활동에) 가담하다

to allow yourself or another person to have something enjoyableand not to mind if they behave badly

industrialist ▫ 산업주의자, 자본가, 경영자, 실업가

a person who owns or runs a factory or industrial company

industry ▫ 근면, 노력, 산업, 공업, 사업, 기업

the large-scale production of goods or of substances such as coal and steel ; businesses that produce a particular type of thing or provide a particular service ; the fact of working hard

ineffective ▫ 쓸모없는, 무효의, 효과가 없는, 무능한, 무력한

something that is ineffective does not achieve what it is intended to achieve

inexplicable	2012 상반기 지방직 9급 불가해한, 설명할 수 없는 not able to be explained or understood
infant	2013 서울특별시, 2006 중앙선거관리위원회 9급 유아, 소아, 갓난아기 ; 유아의 a baby or very young child ; intended for babies or very young children
infanticide	2006 중앙인사위원회 9급 유아 살해 the crime of killing a child
inflammation	2008 상반기 지방직 9급, 2006 중앙인사위원회 9급 염증 swelling and pain in part of your body, which is often red and feels hot
inflict	2011 법원행정처 9급, 2008 하반기 지방직 9급 (괴로움 등을) 가하다[안기다] to force someone to experience something very unpleasant
inhabitant	2013 제1회 지방직 9급 주민 The inhabitants of a place are the people who live there.
initially	2006 서울시 9급 처음에 at the beginning
initiative	2006 중앙선거관리위원회 9급 주도(권), 시작, 독창력 the ability to make decisions and take action without waiting for someone to tell you what to do
injection	2006 서울시 9급, 2005 중앙인사위원회 9급 주입, 주사 an act of putting a drug into someone's body using a special needle ; the act of forcing a liquid into something
injury	2011 상반기 지방직 9급, 2006 중앙인사위원회 9급, 2006 서울시 9급 부상, 상처, 명예 훼손, 손상 a wound or damage to part of your body caused by an accident or attack

innovative	혁신적인

2014 법원사무직 9급

innovative — 혁신적인

an innovative idea or way of doing something is new, different, and better than those that existed before ; using clever new ideas and methods

2005 국회사무처 8급

innumerable — 셀 수 없이 많은, 무수한(=countless)

very many, or too many to be counted

2006 중앙선거관리위원회 9급

inscription — 비명, 비문

a piece of writing inscribed on a stone, in the front of a book, etc.

2013 안전행정부 9급

insecure — 자신이 없는, 불안정한, 위태로운, 걱정스러운

not feeling at all confident about yourself, your abilities, or your relationships with people ; a job, investment, etc. that is insecure does not give you a feeling of safety, because it might to be taken away or lost at any time ; a building or structure that is insecure is not safe, because it could fall down

2005 국회사무처 8급

insignificant — 중요하지 않은, 대수롭지 않은, 하찮은, 무의미한

too small or unimportant to consider or worry about

2013 안전행정부 9급, 2005 국회사무처 8급

insistent — 강요하는, 우기는, 끈질긴

demanding firmly and repeatedly that something should happen

2010 행정안전부 9급

insolvent — 파산한, 지불불능자

unable to pay debts owed, relating to bankruptcy

2005 국회사무처 8급

insomnia — 불면증(=sleeplessness)

if you suffer from insomnia, you are not able to sleep

2013 안전행정부, 2006 중앙선거관리위원회 9급

inspire — 고무하다, 격려하다, (사상 · 감정을) 불어넣다, 영감을 주다

to encourage someone by making them feel confident and eager to do something ; to make someone have a particular feeling or react in a particular way

instruction	2014 안전행정부 9급 교수, 교육, 교훈, 훈령, 명령 the written information that tells you how to do or use something ; a statement telling someone what they must do ; teaching that you are given in a particular skill or subject
insulation	2008 하반기 지방직 9급, 2005 국회사무처 8급 절연(체), 절연물, 단열재 when something is insulated or someone insulates something ; material used to insulate something, especially a building
insult	2006 서울시 9급 모욕 ; 모욕하다 a remark or action that is offensive or deliberately rude ; to offend someone by saying or doing something they think is rude
intensify	2012 행정안전부 9급 (정도 · 강도가) 심해지다[격렬해지다], 강화하다 to become greater, more serious or more extreme, or to make something do this
intensive	2012 하반기 지방직 9급 강한, 격렬한, 집중적인, 집약적인 involving a lot of activity, effort, or careful attention in a short period of time ; farming which produces a lot of food from a small area of land
interaction	2014 서울시 9급 상호 작용 a process by which two or more things affect each other ; the activity of talking to other people, working together with them, etc.
interbreed	2005 중앙인사위원회 9급 이종 교배하다, 이종 교배시키다 to produce young animals from parents of different breeds or groups
interfere	2016 인사혁신처, 2016 지방직 9급 방해하다, 훼방하다, (이해 등이) 대립하다, 간섭하다 to deliberately get involved in a situation where you are not wanted or needed

interpret	2006 중앙선거관리위원회 9급
	해석하다, 설명하다
	to translate spoken words from one language into another ; to explain the meaning of something

interruption	2006 서울시 9급
	중단, 방해
	an act of delaying or interrupting the continuity

intimacy	2012 상반기 지방직 9급
	친밀함, 친밀감을 나타내는 말, 성행위
	when you have a close friendship or sexual relationship with someone

intrepid	2006 서울시 9급
	대담한, 무서움을 모르는
	willing to do dangerous things or go to dangerous places — often used humorously

intriguing	2006 중앙인사위원회 9급
	흥미를 자아내는, 호기심을 자극하는
	something that is intriguing is very interesting because it is strange, mysterious, or unexpected

introduction	2015 인사혁신처 9급
	소개, 서론, 입문, 도입
	the act of bringing something into use for the first time ; the act of bringing something somewhere for the first time

intuition	2012 상반기 지방직 9급, 2009 행정안전부 9급
	직관력, 직감
	Immediate cognition without the use of conscious or rational processes

invariably	2008 상반기 지방직 9급
	변함[예외]없이, 언제나
	in an inevitable manner; not varying at all, always

investment	2013 안전행정부, 2006 서울시 9급
	투자
	to buy shares, property, or goods because you hope that the value will increase and you can make a profit

inverted	2010 행정안전부 9급
	반대의, 반전된, 동성애의, 성도착의
	to turn something upside down or change the order of two things

invigorating	2008 하반기 지방직 9급 기운 나게 하는,(공기·미풍 등이) 상쾌한 giving strength, energy and vitality	
inviting	2009 행정안전부 9급 초대하는, 권유하는, 남의 눈을 끄는, 유혹적인 something that is inviting is very attractive and makes you want to be near it, try it, taste it, etc.	
involve	2006 중앙인사위원회 9급 포함하다, 수반하다 if an activity or situation involves something, that thing is part of it or a result of it	
involved	2015 제1회 지방직 9급, 2005 대구시 9급 (사건 등에) 깊이 관련된, 말려든, (정치·예술 운동 등에) 열심인, 참여하는 to take part in an activity or event, or be connected with it in some way	
irrelevant	2016 인사혁신처 9급 관련이 없는, 무관한, 상관없는 If you describe something such as a fact or remark as irrelevant, you mean that it is not connected with what you are discussing or dealing with.	
isle	2013 제1회 지방직 9급 (작은) 섬 a word for an island, used in poetry or in names of islands	
jackal	2005 대구시 9급 자칼(여우와 늑대의 중간형 야생개) a wild animal like a dog that lives in Asia and Africa and eats the remaining parts of dead animals	
jealousy	2006 중앙선거관리위원회 9급 질투(심) a feeling of being jealous	
jeopardize	2009 상반기 지방직 9급, 2006 중앙인사위원회 9급 위태롭게 하다, 위험하게 하다 to risk losing or spoiling something important	
jurisdiction	2006 중앙인사위원회 9급 관할 지역, 사법권(이 미치는 범위) the right to use an official power to make legal decisions, or the area where this right exists	

justice	2014 법원사무직 9급, 2006 중앙선거관리위원회 9급 정의, 공정, 정당(성) fairness in the way people are treated ; the quality of being right and deserving fair treatment
kinship	2006 중앙인사위원회 9급 혈족 관계, 친척 관계 a family relationship
knowledge	2015 제1회 지방직 9급, 2013 안전행정부, 2006 서울시 9급 지식, 학식 the information, skills, and understanding that you have gained through learning or experience
lamentable	2006 중앙인사위원회 9급 슬픈, 유감스러운, 탄식할 very unsatisfactory or disappointing
landlord	2008 하반기 지방직 9급 주인, 집주인, 지주(=landowner) a man who rents a room, building, or piece of land to someone ; a man who owns or manages a pub
leave	2015 제1회 지방직 9급, 2013 제1회 지방직 떠나다, 두고 가다, 방치하다, 위탁하다 to go away from a place or a person ; to let something remain in a particular state, position, or condition
leftover	2008 하반기 지방직 9급 (식사 후에) 남은 음식, (과거의) 잔재[유물] something that has not been used or eaten when the other parts have been ; the act of getting a title or right after the person who had that title, a series of people or things that come one after the other
likelihood	2016 인사혁신처 9급 가능성, (어떤 일이 있을) 공산 The likelihood of something happening is how likely it is to happen.
likely	2015 사회복지직 9급 있음직한, 가능하다고 생각되는, 정말 같은, ~할 것 같은 suitable for a particular purpose ; something that is likely will probably happen or is probably true
limited	2006 서울시 9급 (수·양 등이) 한정된 not very great in amount, number, ability, etc.

lonely	2012 상반기 지방직 9급, 2005 대구시 9급
	고독한, 쓸쓸한
	a lonely experience or situation makes you unhappy because you are alone or do not have anyone to talk to ; a lonely place is a long way from where people live and very few people go there
loose	2006 중앙선거관리위원회 9급
	헐렁한, 느슨한, 풀린
	not firmly fastened in place ; not tied or fastened very tightly
loquacious	2005 중앙인사위원회 9급
	말이 많은, 수다스러운
	a loquacious person likes to talk a lot
lord	2010 행정안전부 9급
	주(보통 the lord), 장, 지배자, 주인, [영국] 귀족
	a man who has power and authority, a man who ruled over a large area of land in the Middle Ages, used as a name for God or Jesus Christ
lucrative	2015 사회복지직 9급, 2006 중앙선거관리위원회 9급
	유리한, 이익이 있는, 수지맞는, 돈벌이가 되는(=profit-making, money-making, profitable)
	a job or activity that is lucrative lets you earn a lot of money
lustrous	2006 중앙선거관리위원회 9급
	광택이 있는, 윤이 나는, (업적 등이) 훌륭한
	shining in a soft, gentle way
luxuriant	2009 상반기 지방직 9급
	(식물·머리카락이 보기 좋게) 무성한, 풍성한, (특히 예술·분위기에 대해 써서) 풍부한
	thick and healthy hair, having an appealingly rich quality
magnanimous	2006 서울시 9급
	관대한, 도량이 넓은
	kind and generous, especially to someone that you have defeated
maintain	2015 서울특별시 9급
	지속하다, 유지하다, 주장하다, 단언하다
	to make something continue in the same way or at the same standard as before ; to strongly express your belief that something is true

malignancy

2006 중앙선거관리위원회 9급

악의, 적의, 증오, 악성 종양

a feeling of great hatred ; a tumor

mammal

2014 제1차 순경

포유동물

a type of animal that drinks milk from its mother's body when it is young. Humans, dogs, and whales are mammals.

manage

2013 제1회 지방직

이럭저럭 ~해내다, 용케 ~해내다, 경영하다, 단속하다

to direct or control a business or department and the people, equipment, and money involved in it ; to succeed in doing something difficult, especially after trying very hard

manic depression

2005 국회사무처 8급

조울증

a mental illness that causes someone to feel very strong emotions of happiness and sadness in a short period of time

manifest

2007 행정자치부 9급

(특히 감정 · 태도 · 특질을 분명히) 나타내다, 분명해지다

to show plainly ; to make to appear distinctly

manipulate

2016 서울특별시 9급

조종하다, 조작하다, 다루다

If you say that someone manipulates people, you disapprove of them because they skilfully force or persuade people to do what they want.

marginal

2005 국회사무처 8급

가장자리의, 한계의, 최저한의, 빠듯한

a marginal change or difference is too small to be important ; relating to a change in cost, value, etc. when one more thing is produced, one more dollar is earned, etc.

marked

2005 국회사무처 8급

현저한, 두드러진(= striking)

very easy to notice

masculine

2006 서울시 9급

남자의, 남성의, 남자다운

having qualities considered to be typical of men or of what men do

matchless
2008 행정안전부 9급
비할 데 없는, 독보적인
having no mate or match and better than everything else

material
2015 사회복지직 9급, 2013 제1회 지방직, 2005 대구시 9급
물질, 재료, 용구, 자료, 인격적 요소 ; 물질적인, 물질의, 구체적인
cloth used for making clothes, curtains, etc. ; a solid substance such as wood, plastic, or metal ; information or ideas used in books, films, etc. ; relating to your money, possessions, living conditions, etc., rather than the needs of your mind or soul

matricide
2006 중앙인사위원회 9급
모친 살해
the crime of murdering your mother

mature
2014 사회복지직 9급, 2006 중앙선거관리위원회 9급
성숙하다 ; 성숙한
to become fully grown or developed ; to become sensible and start to behave reasonably and sensibly, like an adult ; someone, especially a child or young person, who is mature behaves in a sensible and reasonable way, as you would expect an adult to behave

measure
2015 제1회 지방직 9급
재다, 측정하다, ~의 치수를 재다
to find the size, length, or amount of something, using standard units such as inches, meters, etc.

mechanical
2005 국회사무처 8급
기계(상)의, 기계적인
affecting or involving a machine ; using power from an engine or machine to do a particular kind of work

meditate
2006 중앙선거관리위원회 9급
명상하다, 묵상하다, 꾀하다, 계획하다
to think seriously and deeply about something ; to spend time sitting in a silent, calm state, in order to relax completely or for religious purposes ; to plan to do something, usually something unpleasant

meditation
2006 중앙선거관리위원회 9급
명상, 심사숙고, 고찰, 명상록
the practice of emptying your mind of thoughts and feelings, in order to relax completely or for religious reasons ; the act of thinking deeply and seriously about something

migraine

편두통

an extremely bad headache, during which you feel sick and have pain behind your eyes

mill

(곡물을) 맷돌로 갈다, (제분기[물방아, 기계]로) 빻다 ; 제조 공장, 물방앗간, 제분소

to crush grain, pepper, etc. in a mill ; a building containing a large machine for crushing grain into flour ; a factory that produces materials such as cotton, cloth, or steel

mind

꺼리다

to feel annoyed or upset about something

mineral

광물, 광석

a substance that is formed naturally in the earth, such as coal, salt, stone, or gold. Minerals can be dug out of the ground and used

minute

사소한, 하찮은, 상세한, 미세한

extremely small ; paying careful attention to the smallest details

misappropriate

~을 악용[오용]하다, (남의 돈 등을) 착복하다, 횡령하다

to dishonestly take something that someone has trusted you with, especially money or goods that belong to your employer

misconduct

(공무원 등의) 위법 행위, 직권 남용, (회사의) 부실 경영

bad or dishonest behavior by someone in a position of authority or trust

mission

비행 작전, (우주선에 의한) 특무 비행

an important job that involves travelling somewhere, done by a member of the airforce, army, etc., or by a spacecraft

mitigate

완화하다, (형벌 등을) 가볍게 하다, 경감[완화] 시키다

to make a situation or the effects of something less unpleasant, harmful, or serious
to make something less severe, harmful, or painful

mobility	2005 중앙인사위원회 9급 이동성, (주민의 주소·직업 등의) 유동, 이동 the ability to move easily from one job, area, or social class to another ; the ability to move easily
moderation	2006 중앙인사위원회 9급 중도, 온건, 절제 control of your behavior, so that you keep your actions, feelings, habits, etc. within reasonable limits
modification	2006 중앙선거관리위원회 9급 (부분적) 변경, 변형 a small change made in something such as a design, plan, or system
mold	2009 행정안전부 9급 곰팡이, 사상균 ; 곰팡이가 나다, 곰팡이가 나게 하다 a soft green, grey, or black substance that grows on food which has been kept too long, and on objects that are in warm, wet air
molt	2011 행정안전부 9급 (새가)털을 갈다, (곤충 등이)허물 벗다, (동물이)뿔을 갈다, 털갈이, 털갈이 시기, 벗은 허물 to shed old feathers, hair, or skin, to make way for a new growth.
moment	2013 제1회 지방직 순간, 잠깐 (동안), (어느 특정한) 때, 중요(성) a particular point in time ; a very short period of time
moniker	2006 서울시 9급 이름, 별명 a name, especially one that you choose for yourself or give something — used humorously
monitor	2013 안전행정부 9급, 2005 국회사무처 8급 감시하다, 청취하다 to carefully watch and check a situation in order to see how it changes over a period of time ; to secretly listen to other people's telephone calls, foreign radio broadcasts, etc.
morale	2006 중앙인사위원회 9급 사기, 의욕 the level of confidence and positive feelings that people have, especially people who work together, who belong to the same team, etc.

motherhood	2006 중앙인사위원회 9급 어머니임, 모성(애) the state of being a mother
muscle	2015 제1회 지방직 9급, 2013 안전행정부 근육, 완력, 깡패 one of the pieces of flesh inside your body that you use in order to move, and that connect your bones together ; physical strength and power
myriad	2006 중앙인사위원회 9급 수많은, 무수한, 막대한 very many
myth	2015 제1회 지방직 9급, 2005 국회사무처 8급 신화(神話), 사회적 통념(通念), 꾸며낸 이야기 an idea or story that many people believe, but which is not true ; an ancient story, especially one invented in order to explain natural or historical events
mythical	2005 중앙인사위원회 9급 신화의, 신화적인, 상상적인, 가공의 existing only in an ancient story ; imagined or invented
naive	2008 행정안전부 9급 (경험·지식 부족 등으로) 순진해 빠진, (모자랄 정도로) 순진무구한 having or showing a lack of experience or knowledge
namelessness	2012 상반기 지방직 9급 무명, 서출(庶出)임, 형언할 수 없음 having no name or no known name, difficult to describe, a child illegitimate
NASA	2005 국회사무처 8급 미 항공 우주국(National Aeronautics and Space Administration) a US government organization that controls space travel and the scientific study of space
nasty	2009 행정안전부 9급 (아주 나빠서) 끔찍한, (성격·행동 등이) 못된, 위험한, 심각한, 추잡한 highly unpleasant or repugnant, physically or mentally damaging or harmful
nationality	2005 대구시 9급 국적, 국민(성), 민족, 국가 the state of being legally a citizen of a particular country ; a large group of people with the same race, origin, language, etc.

natural selection

2005 중앙인사위원회 9급

자연 도태

the process by which only plants and animals that are naturally suitable for life in their environment will continue to live and breed, while all others will die out

nature

2013 안전행정부

천성, 성질, (사물의) 본질, 자연

someone's character ; everything in the physical world that is not controlled by humans, such as wild plants and animals, earth and rocks, and the weather

nearby

2013 서울특별시

가까운 ; 가까이로, 가까이에, 근처에

not far away

necessity

2014 법원사무직

필수품, 불가결한 것, 필요(성), 필연(성)

something that you need to have in order to live ; when something is necessary

neglect

2013 제1회 지방직

무시하다, (무관심 · 부주의 등으로) ~하지 않다, (의무 · 일 등을) 게을리 하다 ; 태만, 무시

to fail to look after someone or something properly ; to pay too little attention to something ; to not do something

negotiate

2015 제1회 지방직 9급

협상하다, 교섭하다, (교섭으로) 협정하다

to discuss something in order to reach an agreement, especially in business or politics

nervous

2013 안전행정부, 2005 대구시 9급

긴장한, 초조한, 자신 없는

worried or frightened about something, and unable to relax ; often becoming worried or frightened, and easily upset

neuron

2006 중앙선거관리위원회 9급

뉴런(신경 단위)

a type of cell that makes up the nervous system and sends messages to other parts of the body or the brain

nomadic

2006 중앙선거관리위원회 9급

유목의, 방랑의

nomadic people are nomads

nominal	2012 상반기 지방직 9급 명목상의, 이름뿐인, (돈의 액수가) 아주 적은, (문법) 명사의 in name or thought but not reality
nonetheless	2006 서울시 9급 그럼에도 불구하고 in spite of the fact that has just been mentioned
notably	2005 국회사무처 8급 현저하게, 두드러지게, 명백하게, 특히 used to say that a person or thing is a typical example or the most important example of something ; in a way that is clearly different, important, or unusual
nuisance	2008 행정안전부 9급 성가신[귀찮은] 사람[것/일], 골칫거리, (법의 제지를 받을 수 있는) 소란[방해] 행위 a person or thing causing inconvenience or annoyance
numberless	2005 국회사무처 8급 이루 다 셀 수 없는, 셀 수 없이 많은, 무수한 too many to be counted
nurture	2013 제1회 지방직 9급 양육, 교육, 후천성, 음식물 ; (아이를) 양육하다, 기르다, 양성하다 the education and care that you are given as a child, and the way it affects your later development and attitudes ; to feed and take care of a child or a plant while it is growing ; to help a plan, idea, feeling, etc. to develop
nutrition	2013 안전행정부 9급 영양물 섭취, 영양물, 음식물, 영양학 the process of giving or getting the right type of food for good health and growth ; the science that deals with the effects of food, vitamins, etc. on people's health
obligation	2006 중앙선거관리위원회 9급 의무, 책임, 구속, 채권 관계 a moral or legal duty to do something
obscene	2013 안전행정부 음란한, 외설스러운, 풍기를 문란케 하는 relating to sex in a way that is shocking and offensive ; extremely unfair, immoral, or unpleasant, especially in a way that makes you angry

	2005 대구시 9급
obstacle	장애(물), 방해(물) something that makes it difficult to achieve something ; an object which blocks your way, so that you must try to go around it
	2013 제1회 지방직 9급
obvious	명백한, 명확한, 눈에 잘 띄는 easy to notice or understand

 Example The _____ way of reducing pollution is to use cars less.

📄 obvious

	2015 제1회 지방직 9급
obviously	분명히, 명백히, 두드러지게, 눈에 띄게 used to mean that a fact can easily be noticed or understood
	2014 법원사무직 9급
occasion	(특정한) 경우, 때, 기회, 특별한 일, 행사 a time when something happens ; a suitable or favourable time ; an important social event or ceremony
	2006 중앙선거관리위원회 9급
occasionally	때때로, 가끔 sometimes, but not regularly and not often
	2010 행정안전부 9급
onward	앞으로[계속 이어서] 나아가는 moving forward to a later time or a more distant place
	2010 서울시 9급
opposite	정반대의 일[사람, 말] ; 반대편의, 정반대의 a person or thing that is as different as possible from someone or something else ; as different as possible from something else ; the opposite direction, way, etc. is directly away from someone or something
	2006 중앙인사위원회 9급
organism	유기체, 생물, 인간 a system made up of parts that are dependent on each other ; an animal, plant, human, or any other living thing

orgy	2009 행정안전부 9급 진탕 먹고 마시며 난잡하게 노는 잔치, ~을 미친 듯이 해댐 a wild party characterized by excessive drinking and indiscriminate sexual activity, a period of excessive indulgence in a specified activity
ornament	2006 중앙인사위원회 9급 장식, 장식품 decoration that is added to something ; a small object that you keep in your house because it is beautiful rather than useful
oust	2006 중앙인사위원회 9급 내쫓다 to force someone out of a position of power, especially so that you can take their place
outbreak	2013 서울시 9급 (전쟁·질병 등의) 발발, 돌발, 폭동 if there is an outbreak of fighting or disease in an area, it suddenly starts to happen
outburst	2005 중앙인사위원회 9급 (화산·격정 등의) 폭발, 분출 something you say suddenly that expresses a strong emotion, especially anger
outgrowth	2005 중앙인사위원회 9급 자연적인 발전[결과, 소산], 파생물, 부산물 something that develops from something else, as a natural result of it ; something that grows out of something else
outline	2005 국회사무처 8급 윤곽, 약도, 개요, 요점 the main ideas or facts about something, without the details
outnumber	2012 상반기 지방직 9급 ~보다 수가 더 많다, 수적으로 우세하다 to be greater in number than someone or something
outspoken	2010 행정안전부 9급 (남의 기분에 신경 쓰지 않고) 노골적으로[거침없이] 말하는 talking in a free and honest way about your opinions
outstanding	2017 인사혁신처 두드러진, 현저한, 우수한 extremely good ; very great or clear

overall

2013 안전행정부 9급

전부의, 총체적인, 포괄적인 ; 작업 바지, 작업복

considering or including everything ; heavy cotton trousers with a piece covering your chest, held up by pieces of cloth that go over your shoulders

override

2005 국회사무처 8급

(결정 등을) 무효로 하다, 번복하다

to use your power or authority to change someone else's decision

overwhelm

2013 서울시 9급, 2005 국회사무처 8급

압도하다, 당황하게 하다

if someone is overwhelmed by an emotion, they feel it so strongly that they cannot think clearly ; to surprise someone very much, so that they do not know how to react

---

 Example Harriet was _____ by a feeling of homesickness.
📖 overwhelmed

---

overwhelming

2006 중앙인사위원회 9급, 2006 중앙선거관리위원회 9급

압도적인, 불가항력의, 굉장한, 극도의

having such a great effect on you that you feel confused and do not know how to react ; very large or greater, more important, etc. than any other

palatable

2008 행정안전부 9급

맛있는, 마음에 드는, 구미에 맞는

pleasant to taste, acceptable of an action or proposal

parallel

2005 국회사무처 8급

평행선, 유사(물), 필적하는 것

a relationship or similarity between two things, especially things that exist or happen in different places or at different times

part

2013 제1회 지방직

(연극의) 등장인물, 역, 대사, 대본, 임무, 역할

the words and actions of a particular character in a play or film

particular

2015 인사혁신처 9급, 2013 서울특별시 9급

특별한, 특유의, 특수한

a particular thing or person is the one that you are talking about, and not any other ; special or great

partisan	2006 중앙인사위원회 9급
	당파적인, 당파심이 강한
	strongly supporting a particular political party, plan or leader, usually without considering the other choices carefully
pathway	2012 상반기 지방직 9급, 2006 중앙선거관리위원회 9급
	통로, 경로, (사람만이 다닐 수 있는) 좁은 길, 오솔길, (생화학) 경로
	a track which a person can walk along, a set of connected chemical reactions in biology ; a path : a series of nerves that pass information to each other
patricide	2006 중앙인사위원회 9급
	부친 살해
	the crime of murdering your father
peasant	2006 중앙선거관리위원회 9급
	농부, 소작인, 소작농
	a poor farmer who owns or rents a small amount of land, either in past times or in poor countries
peer	2014 안전행정부 9급, 2008 행정안전부 9급
	(나이 · 지위 · 능력이) 동등한 사람, (가치 · 질이) 동등한 것, (영국의) 귀족, (나이 · 신분이 같거나 비슷한) 또래[동배]
	your peers are the people who are the same age as you, or who have the same type of job, social class, etc. ; a member of the British nobility
peerage	2006 중앙인사위원회 9급
	귀족, 귀족 사회
	the rank of a British peer ; all the British peers considered as a group
penalize	2010 상반기 지방직 9급
	(법 · 규칙을 어긴 데 대해) 처벌하다, (부당한 처사로 사람을) 불리하게 만들다
	to cause someone a disadvantage, to punish someone or somethingfor breaking a rule or a law
penchant	2006 중앙인사위원회 9급
	강한 경향, 취미, 기호(=liking)
	if you have a penchant for something, you like that thing very much and try to do it or have it often
penmanship	2009 행정안전부 9급
	서법, 서도
	the quality or style of someone's handwriting

	2015 제1회 지방직 9급, 2008 하반기 지방직 9급
perception	지각(력), 인식, 이해, 견해
	the way you think about something and your idea of what it is like ; the way that you notice things with your senses of sight, hearing, etc.
	2007 행정자치부 9급
peripherally	주위[주변]에, 말초적으로, 지엽적으로
	not relating to the main or most important part
	2014 서울시 9급
persuade	~을 설득시키다, 믿게 하다, 확인시키다, 납득시키다
	to make someone decide to do something, especially by giving them reasons why they should do it, or asking them many times to do it ; to make someone believe something or feel sure about something
	2005 국회사무처 8급
persuasion	설득, 권유, 신념, 신조, 종파
	the act of persuading someone to do something ; a particular type of belief, especially a political or religious one
	2006 중앙선거관리위원회 9급
petition	탄원(서), 청원(서), 신청(서)
	a written request signed by a lot of people, asking someone in authority to do something or change something ; an official letter to a law court, asking for a legal case to be considered
	2006 서울시 9급
petty	작은, 사소한, 마음이 좁은, 인색한
	a petty problem, detail etc is small and unimportant ; unkind and caring too much about small unimportant things
	2005 국회사무처 8급
philosophical	철학의, 철학적인, 철학자다운
	relating to philosophy
	2005 중앙인사위원회 9급
philosophize	철학적으로 설명[사색]하다
	to talk about serious subjects in detail or for a long time
	2010 상반기 지방직 9급
pictorial	그림을 이용한, 그림이 포함된, 그림[회화]의
	relating to painting or drawing

pitch	2005 국회사무처 8급 음조, 음의 고저 how high or low a note or other sound is
pitfall	2010 상반기 지방직 9급 (눈에 잘 안 띄는) 위험[곤란] a likely mistake or problem in a situation
pleased	2013 안전행정부 · 서울특별시, 2005 대구시 9급 기쁜, 만족스러운 happy or satisfied
pleasure	2011 행정안전부 9급 즐거움, 유쾌함, 만족, 기쁨 the feeling of happiness, enjoyment, or satisfaction that you get from an experience
plight	2009 행정안전부 9급 역경, 곤경, 맹세, 약혼 a dangerous, difficult, or otherwise unfortunate situation, be engaged to be married to
plumbing	2008 하반기 지방직 9급 (건물의) 배관[수도 시설], 배관 작업[공사] the water pipes and similar systems in a building
plummet	2015 인사혁신처 9급, 2010 상반기 지방직 9급 곤두박질치다, 급락하다 to fall very quickly and suddenly
pointless	2005 대구시 9급 뾰족한 끝이 없는, 무딘, 효과가 없는, 무의미한, 적절하지 못한 worthless or not likely to have any useful result
poker	2005 중앙인사위원회 9급 부지깽이 a metal stick used to move coal or wood in a fire to make it burn better
policymaker	2005 국회사무처 8급 정책 입안[수립]자, 정책 결정자 someone who decides what an organization's or government's policies will be
polish	2005 대구시 9급 ~을 닦다, ~의 윤[광]을 내다 to make something smooth, bright, and shiny by rubbing it

pollutant	2013 지방직 9급
	오염 물질, 오염원, 오염
	a substance that makes air, water, soil, etc. dangerously dirty, and is caused by cars, factories, etc.
population	2015 인사혁신처 9급
	인구, 주민(수), 개체군, 개체수
	the number of people living in a particular area, country, etc. ; all of the people who live in a particular area
pose	2014 법원사무직 9급, 2005 국회사무처 8급
	(문제 · 주장 등을) 제기하다, 자세[포즈]를 취하게 하다[취하다]
	to ask a question, especially one that needs to be carefully thought about ; to sit or stand in a particular position in order to be photographed or painted, or to make someone do this
possess	2015 서울특별시 9급, 2006 중앙선거관리위원회 9급
	(감정 · 관념 등이) 지배하다, 마음을 사로잡다
	if a feeling possesses you, you suddenly feel it very strongly and it affects your behavior
potential	2015 서울특별시 9급, 2013 안전행정부 9급, 2006 중앙인사위원회 9급
	잠재(능)력, 가능성 ; 잠재적인, 발전 가능성이 있는, 잠재력이 있는, 가능한
	if people or things have potential, they have a natural ability or quality that could develop to make them very good ; the possibility that something will develop in a particular way, or have a particular effect ; likely to develop into a particular type of person or thing in the future
practical	2016 · 2015 서울특별시 9급
	실행할 수 있는, 사용할 수 있는, 실용적인
	relating to real situations and events rather than ideas, emotions, etc.
prairie	2008 행정안전부 9급
	(북미 · 캐나다의) 대초원
	a large, mostly flat area of land in North America that has few trees and is covered in grasses
precede	2014 제1회 지방직 9급
	앞서다, 앞장서다, ~의 윗자리를 차지하다, ~보다 우월하다
	to go somewhere before someone else ; to happen or exist before something or someone, or to come before something else in a series

precedence

2012 상반기 지방직 9급

우선(함)

the condition of preceding others in importance, order, or rank

precipitation

2016 지방직 9급

강수량

Precipitation is rain, snow, or hail.

precision

2015 제1회 지방직 9급, 2010 행정안전부 9급

정확(성), 정밀(성), 신중함

the quality, condition, or fact of being precise

predict

2015 인사혁신처 9급

예언하다, 예측하다, 예보하다(=foretell)

to say that something will happen, before it happens

Example Newspapers _____ that Davis would be re-elected.

predicted

---

pre-existing

2006 중앙선거관리위원회 9급

기존의

existing before a particular time or event

prehistoric

2006 중앙선거관리위원회 9급

유사(有史) 이전의, 선사(先史)의

relating to the time in history before anything was written down

pregnant

2006 중앙인사위원회 9급

임신한

if a woman or female animal is pregnant, she has an unborn baby growing inside her body

preponderance

2011 행정안전부 9급

(수적으로) 우세함[더 많음]

greater amount or number of something

prerequisite

2010 행정안전부 9급

(무엇이 있기 위해서는 꼭 필요한) 전제 조건

something that you officially must have or do before you can have or do something

prerogative

2006 중앙선거관리위원회 9급

특권을 가진 ; 특권

a right that someone has, especially because of their importance or social position

prescient	2005 국회사무처 8급 미리 아는, 앞을 내다보는, 선견지명이 있는 able to imagine or know what will happen in the future
prescribe	2015 제1회 지방직 9급, 2009 상반기 지방직 9급, 2005 국회사무처 8급 규정하다, 명령하다, 지시하다, 처방하다 to state officially what should be done in a particular situation ; to say what medicine or treatment a sick person should have
preservation	2005 중앙인사위원회 9급 보존, 유지, 보호, 보관, 저장, 예방 when something is kept in its original state or in good condition ; the act of making sure that a situation continues without changing
preserve	2014 법원사무직 9급 보호하다, 보존하다, 유지하다, 저장하다 to save something or someone from being harmed or destroyed ; to make something continue without changing ; to store food for a long time after treating it so that it will not decay
presidency	2012 상반기 지방직 9급 대통령직[임기], 회장직[임기] the job of a president or the period of time when a person is president
prevalent	2006 중앙인사위원회 9급 널리 퍼진 common at a particular time, in a particular place, or among a particular group of people
prevent	2015 사회복지직 9급 막다, 방해하다, 예방하다, 방지하다 to stop something from happening, or stop someone from doing something
previous	2006 중앙인사위원회 9급 이전의 having happened or existed before the event, time, or thing that you are talking about now

previously

2005 국회사무처 8급

이전에, 미리

before now or before a particular time

 Almost half the group had _____ been heavy smokers.

📖 previously

primitive

2006 중앙인사위원회 9급

원시의, 옛날의, 미개의

belonging to a simple way of life that existed in the past and does not have modern parts that would make it faster, better, more comfortable, etc.

priority

2008 행정안전부 9급

먼저임, (중요도 · 긴급도에서의) 상위, 우위, 상석, 우선권

the thing that you think is most important and that needs attention before anything else ; the right to be given attention first and before other people or things

prize

2006 중앙인사위원회 9급

목적(물), 상, 상품

something that is given to someone who is successful in a competition, race, game of chance, etc. ; something that is very valuable to you or that it is very important to have

prodigal

2016 서울특별시 9급

(돈 · 시간 · 에너지 · 물자를) 낭비하는

You can describe someone as a prodigal son or daughter if they leave their family or friends, often after a period of behaving badly, and then return at a later time as a better person.

productive

2006 서울시 9급, 2005 대구시 9급

생산적인, 다산의, 풍부한, 영리적인

producing or achieving a lot ; relating to the production of goods, crops, or wealth

profit

2015 사회복지직 9급, 2013 안전행정부, 2006 중앙선거관리위원회 9급

도움이 되다, 얻는 바가 있다

to be useful or helpful to someone

profound

2014 법원사무직 9급, 2005 중앙인사위원회 9급

깊은, 심원한, 뜻 깊은, 난해한

having a strong influence or effect ; showing strong, serious feelings ; showing great knowledge and understanding

profuse

풍부한, 많은, 다량의

Profuse sweating, bleeding, or vomiting is sweating, bleeding, or vomiting large amounts.

prolific

다작하는, 다산하는

A prolific writer, artist, or composer produces a large number of works.

promote

증진하다, 촉진하다, 장려하다, 승진시키다

to help something to develop or increase

prop

지주, 버팀목, 받침대, (연극 · 영화에 쓰이는) 소품

a pole or beam used as a temporary support, a major source of support or assistance.

propel

(몰거나 밀거나 해서) 나아가게 하다, (사람을 특정한 방향 · 상황으로) 몰고 가다

to push or move something somewhere with a lot of force, to cause someone to do an activity or be in a situation

property

재산, 소유물, 상품, 부동산

the thing or things that someone owns

prophecy

예언, 예언 능력, 신의(神意)의 전달, 예언서

a statement that something will happen in the future, especially one made by someone with religious or magic powers ; the power or act of making statements about what will happen in the future

protective

지키는, 보호하는, 방어하는

used or intended for protection ; wanting to protect someone from harm or danger

proud

거만한, 잘난 체하는, 자존심이 있는, 자랑으로 여기는

having respect for yourself, so that you are embarrassed to ask for help when you are in a difficult situation ; feeling pleased about something that you have done or something that you own, or about someone or something you are involved with or related to

proxy

2006 중앙인사위원회 9급

대리 행위, 대리 투표, 대리인

if you do something by proxy, you arrange for someone else to do it for you ; someone who you choose to represent you, especially to vote for you

pseudonym

2006 서울시 9급

(작가의) 필명, 가명, 익명

an invented name that a writer, artist, etc. uses instead of their real name

psychiatric

2005 국회사무처 8급

정신의학의, 정신과의

relating to the study and treatment of mental illness

psychological

2005 국회사무처 8급

심리학의, 심리(학)적인

relating to the way that your mind works and the way that this affects your behavior ; relating to what is in someone's mind rather than what is real

psychologist

2005 국회사무처 8급

심리학자, 정신분석 의사

someone who is trained in psychology

public opinion

2006 중앙인사위원회 9급

여론

the opinions or beliefs that ordinary people have about a particular subject

pull

2013 서울특별시 9급

끌어당기기, 당기는 힘, 인력, 매력

an act of using force to move something towards you or in the same direction that you are moving ; a strong physical force that makes things move in a particular direction ; the ability to attract someone or have a powerful effect on them

---

Example He gave her a sharp _____ forward.

🖉 pull

---

punctuate

2008 상반기 지방직 9급

간간이 끼어들다, (문장에) 구두점을 찍다

to interrupt something repeatedly, to use punctuation marks in a piece of writing

pupil

2008 행정안전부 9급

(특히 어린) 학생, (전문가에게서 배우는) 문하생[제자], 눈동자, 동공

a student under the supervision of a teacher or professor

purist

2005 국회사무처 8급

순수주의자

someone who believes that something should be done in the correct or traditional way, especially in the areas of art, sport, music, and language

quack

2009 행정안전부 9급

돌팔이 의사, (오리가) 꽥꽥 우는 소리, 시끄럽게 지껄이다, 엉터리 치료를 하다

an unqualified person who dishonestly claims to have medical knowledge, the characteristic harsh sound made by a duck

quantity

2011 행정안전부 9급

양

an amount of something that can be counted or measured

questionnaire

2009 상반기 지방직 9급

설문지

a list of questions that several people are asked so that information can be collected about something

raise

2015 제1회 지방직 9급, 2013 안전행정부

기르다, 양육하다, 사육하다

to look after your children and help them grow ; to look after animals or grow plants so that they can be sold or used as food

react

2015 사회복지직 9급

반작용하다, 반동하다, 반항하다, (자극 등에) 반응하다

to behave in a particular way or show a particular emotion because of something that has happened or been said ; if a chemical substance reacts, it changes when it is mixed with another chemical substance

realistic

2013 행정안전부 9급

현실주의의, 현실적인, 진짜 같은, 사실적인

judging and dealing with situations in a practical way according to what is actually possible rather than what you would like to happen ; a realistic aim or hope is one that it is possible to achieve ; realistic pictures or stories show things as they are in real life

2. 기출단어(영영뜻) 181

	2005 대구시 9급
reasoning	추론, 추리, 논증
	a process of thinking carefully about something in order to make a judgment
	2016 서울특별시 9급
rebellious	(규칙·일반 통념 등에 대해) 반항적인
	If you say that someone is defiant, you mean they show aggression or independence by refusing to obey someone.
	2009 상반기 지방직 9급, 2005 대구시 9급
recession	퇴거, 후퇴, (일시적) 경기 후퇴, 불경기
	a difficult time when there is less trade, business activity, etc. in a country than usual
	2012 상반기 지방직 9급
recessive	열성의
	causing or relating to a characteristic or condition that a child will have only if both of the child's parents have it
	2011 행정안전부 9급
recipient	(어떤 것을) 받는 사람, 수령[수취]인
	One who receives, such as one who receives money or goods
	2011 행정안전부 9급
reciprocal	상호간의
	a relationship in which two people or groups agree to do something similar for each other
	2011 행정안전부 9급
reclaim	(분실하거나 빼앗긴 물건 등을) 되찾다, (황무지 등을) 개간하다, (폐품을) 재활용하다, (중독자·범죄자 등을) 갱생시키다
	to take back something that was yours ; to make land, such as desert or areas covered by water, suitable for farming or building ; to treat waste materials in order to get useful materials, such as glass or paper, that can be used again
	2011 행정안전부 9급
reconcilable	조정할[화해시킬] 수 있는, 조화[일치]시킬 수 있는
	to cause people or groups to become friendly again after an argument or disagreement ; to find a way of making two different things exist or be true at the same time

reconcile	2008 행정안전부 9급 (두 가지 이상의 생각·요구 등을) 조화시키다, 화해시키다, (어쩔 수 없는 불쾌한 상황을 체념하고) 받아들이다 to make things compatible or consistent, to accept something unpleasant resignedly
recurrent	2012 상반기 지방직 9급 되풀이되는, 재발되는 occurring often or repeatedly
redeem	2016 인사혁신처 9급 회복하다, 되찾다 If you redeem yourself or your reputation, you do something that makes people have a good opinion of you again after you have behaved or performed badly.
reformer	2005 국회사무처 8급 개혁가, 정치 개혁론자 someone who works to improve a social or political system
regimen	2005 중앙인사위원회 9급 양생법, 식이 요법, 통치, 관리, 지배 a special plan of food, exercise, etc. that is intended to improve your health
regretful	2005 대구시 9급 뉘우치는, 슬퍼하는, 애석해 하는, 유감의 뜻을 표하는 someone who is regretful feels sorry or disappointed
relatives	2016 인사혁신처 9급 친척, 친지 Your relatives are the members of your family.
relatively	2013 안전행정부·제1회 지방직 9급, 2005 국회사무처 8급, 2005 대구시 9급 상대적으로, 비교적, (~에) 비례하여, 비해서(to) something that is relatively small, easy, etc. is fairly small, easy, etc. compared to other things
reliability	2011 행정안전부 9급 확실성, 신뢰성, 신빙성, 신뢰할 수 있음, 신뢰도, 확실성 the quality of being reliable, dependable or trustworthy
reliable	2013 제1회 지방직 믿을 만한, 신뢰성 있는 someone or something that is reliable can be trusted or depended on

relieve	2014 제1차 순경 (고통·중압 등을) 경감하다, ~을 안심시키다, (빈곤·탄압 등에서) 구제하다, 돋보이게 하다 to reduce someone's pain or unpleasant feelings
relieved	2015 제1회 지방직 9급, 2014 제1차 순경, 2005 대구시 9급 안심한, 안도한 feeling happy because you are no longer worried about something
reluctance	2006 중앙선거관리위원회 9급 싫음, 마지못해 함 when someone is unwilling to do something, or when they do something slowly to show that they are not very willing
repair	2014 제1차 순경, 2013 제1회 지방직 9급, 2006 중앙선거관리위원회 9급 수선, 수리 ; 수선하다, 수리하다 something that you do to fix a thing that is damaged, broken, or not working ; to fix something that is damaged, broken, split, or not working properly
replace	2013 안전행정부 제자리에 놓다, 되돌리다, 대신하다, 바꾸다, 교환하다 to put something back where it was before ; to start doing something instead of another person, or start being used instead of another thing ; to remove someone from their job or something from its place, and put a new person or thing there
replicate	2009 행정안전부 9급 (정확히) 모사[복제]하다, 자기 복제를 하다 to make or do something again in exactly the same way
repose	2006 중앙선거관리위원회 9급 휴식(=rest), 한적함, 평화 a state of calm or comfortable rest
reproduction	2015 인사혁신처 9급 재생, 재현, 복제품, 번식 the act of producing a copy of a book, picture, piece of music, etc. ; a copy of a work of art, piece of furniture, etc. ; the act or process of producing babies, young animals, or plants

reptile	2012 하반기 지방직 9급 **파충류 동물, 파행 동물(=crawling animal), 비열한 사람, 악랄한 인간 ; 파행하는, 기어 다니는, 파충류의, 비열한** a type of animal, such as a snake or lizard, whose body temperature changes according to the temperature around it, and that usually lays eggs to have babies ; someone who is unpleasant or cannot be trusted
reputation	2015 제1회 지방직 9급 **평판, 세평, 명성, 호평** the opinion that people have about someone or something because of what has happened in the past
research	2013 안전행정부 9급 **(학술) 연구, 과학적 탐구, 학술 조사, 연구심 ; 연구하다, 조사하다** serious study of a subject, in order to discover new facts or test new ideas ; the activity of finding information about something that you are interested in or need to know about ; to study a subject in detail, especially in order to discover new facts or test new ideas ; to get all the necessary facts and information for something
resentment	2006 서울시 9급 **원한, 분개, 분노** a feeling of anger because something has happened that you think is unfair
resident	2013 안전행정부 **거주자, 거류민, 외국 주재 사무관 ; 사는, 거주하는** someone who lives or stays in a particular place ; living in a place
residue	2012 상반기 지방직 9급 **잔여[잔류]물, 잔여 유산** whatever remains after something else has been removed
resistant	2015 서울특별시 9급 **저항하는, 방지하는, 방해하는, 저항력이 있는** not damaged or affected by something ; opposed to something and wanting to prevent it from happening
resolve	2011 상반기 지방직 9급 **결심하다, 결정하다, 풀다, 해결하다, 분해하다** to make a definite decision to do something ; to find a satisfactory way of dealing with a problem or difficulty

respondent

2009 상반기 지방직 9급

응답자, 설문 참여자

a person who gives a response or answer to a question that is asked especially as part of a survey

resurgence

2016 서울특별시 9급

재기, 부활

If there is a resurgence of an attitude or activity, it reappears and grows.

retain

2007 행정자치부 9급

(계속) 유지[보유]하다, 간직[함유]하다

to keep or continue to have something

retaliation

2006 서울시 9급

(같은 수단으로의) 앙갚음, 보복

action against someone who has done something bad to you

retention

2005 중앙인사위원회 9급

보류, 보유, 유지, 구치, 감금

the act of keeping something ; the ability or tendency of something to hold liquid, heat, etc. within itself

reticent

2005 중앙인사위원회 9급

말이 없는, 과묵한, 말을 삼가는, 입이 무거운

unwilling to talk about what you feel or what you know

retrieve

2015 사회복지직 9급

되찾다, 회수하다, 부활시키다, 만회하다 ; 회복, 회수, 만회

to find something and bring it back

retrospect

2008 행정안전부 9급

회상, 추억, 선례의 참고, 회상에 잠기다, 소급하여 대조해 보다

thinking about the past or something that happened in the past

reveal

2014 안전행정부 9급, 2006 중앙인사위원회 9급

드러내다, 폭로하다

to make known something that was previously secret or unknown ; to show something that was previously hidden

revenge

2006 서울시 9급

복수(심) ; 복수하다

something you do in order to punish someone who has harmed or offended you ; to punish someone who has done something to harm you or someone else

reverence

(~에 대한) 숭상, 존경, 존경심

great respect and admiration for someone or something

review

복습하다, 다시 조사하다, 관찰하다, 회상하다

to look again at something you have studied, such as notes, reports, etc. ; to examine, consider, and judge a situation or process carefully in order to see if changes are necessary

revolve

회전하다, 자전하다, 공전하다, 운행하다

to move around like a wheel, or to make something move around like a wheel ; to move in circles around something

revolt

반란, 폭동(=rebellion, insurgency, tumult)

a refusal to accept someone's authority or obey rules or laws ; strong and often violent action by a lot of people against their ruler or government

------

Example   The prime minister is now facing a _____ by members of his own par

📖 revolt

------

ridden

(복합어를 이루어) ~에 지배된, 억압당한, (악몽 등에) 시달린, 얽매인

very full of something unpleasant

rig

(부정한 수법으로) 조작하다, (배에 선구를) 갖추다, (장비를) 설치[장치]하다.

to arrange dishonestly for the result of something, for example an election, to be changed, to provide (a boat) with sails and rigging

rigid

(규칙·방법·사람 등이) 엄격한, 융통성 없는, (사물·물질이)뻣뻣한, 단단한, 잘 휘지 않는

not able to be bent, moved, changed or persuaded

ritual

종교적인 의식, 의식적인 행사, 예의, 풍습

a ceremony that is always performed in the same way, in order to mark an important religious or social occasion

	2005 대구시 9급
roar	으르렁거리는 소리, 포효, 외치는 소리 ; (짐승 등이) 으르렁거리다, 고함치다, 외치다 a deep, loud noise made by an animal such as a lion, or by someone's voice ; to make a deep, very loud noise ; to shout something in a deep powerful voice
	2005 국회사무처 8급
robbery	강도(질), 도둑질, 약탈 the crime of stealing money or things from a bank, shop, etc., especially using violence

 Police are investigating a series of bank _____ in South Wales.

📖 robberies

	2006 중앙선거관리위원회 9급
robe	길고 헐거운 겉옷, 예복 a long loose piece of clothing, especially one worn for official ceremonies
	2006 서울시 9급
rubric	(책 등의 장·절의) 제명, 제목 a set of instructions or an explanation in a book, examination paper, etc. ; a title under which particular things are mentioned or discussed
	2005 대구시 9급
rumble	(천둥·지진 등이) 우르르 울리다, 덜거덕거리며 가다 to make a series of long low sounds, especially a long distance away from you ; to move slowly along while making a series of long low sounds
	2005 중앙인사위원회 9급
rush	돌진하다, 급하게 가다 to move very quickly, especially because you need to be somewhere very soon
	2008 하반기 지방직 9급
sabotage	(고의적인) 방해행위, 사보타주(*적이 사용하는 것을 막기 위해 또는 무엇에 대한 항의의 표시로 장비, 운송 시설, 기계 등을 고의로 파괴하는 것) to intentionally damage or destroy equipment, weapons, buildings and plans in order to prevent the success of an enemy or competitor.

2006 중앙선거관리위원회 9급

sacred

신성한, 성스러운(=holy)

relating to a god or religion ; very important or greatly respected

2005 국회사무처 8급

safeguard

~을 지키다, 보호하다, 호송하다 ; 보호(책), 보호 수단, 호위병, (기계 등의) 안전장치

to protect something from harm or damage ; a rule, agreement, etc. that is intended to protect someone or something from possible dangers or problems

2005 국회사무처 8급

salvation

구원, 구조, 구출, 구제(자), 구제 수단

something that prevents or saves someone or something from danger, loss, or failure ; in the Christian religion, the state of being saved from evil

Example The Internet turned out to be the ______ of the company.

답 salvation

2015 인사혁신처 9급, 2014 법원사무직 9급, 2005 중앙인사위원회 9급

scale

비늘

one of the small flat pieces of skin that cover the bodies of fish, snakes, etc.

2012 상반기 지방직 9급

scarce

부족한, 드문, 겨우, 거의 ~ 않다

insufficient for the demand

2013 안전행정부, 2006 서울시 9급

scare

공황, 공포

a situation in which a lot of people become frightened about something ; a sudden feeling of fear

2005 중앙인사위원회 9급

scheme

계획, 계략

an official plan that is intended to help people in some way, for example by providing education or training ; a clever plan, especially to do something that is bad or illegal – used in order to show disapproval

schizophrenia	2012 상반기 지방직 9급
	정신 분열증
	a very serious mental illness in which someone cannot think or behave normally and often experiences delusions

scholarly	2005 국회사무처 8급
	학자의, 학재[학구]적인, 박식한, 학문상의, 전문적인
	relating to serious study of a particular subject ; someone who is scholarly spends a lot of time studying, and knows a lot about a particular subject

scope	2011 행정안전부 9급
	(무엇을 하거나 이룰 수 있는) 기회[여지/능력], (주제 · 조직 · 활동 등이 다루는) 범위, (공간의) 넓이, 길이
	the range of a subject covered by a book, program, discussion, class, etc., the opportunity or possibility for doing something

scrape	2006 중앙선거관리위원회 9급
	(돈 · 물건 등을) 긁어모으다
	to make savings through hardship

scrutiny	2009 상반기 지방직 9급
	정밀 조사, 철저한 검토
	critical observation or examination

secure	2011 행정안전부 9급
	안심하는, 안전한, 확실한, 튼튼한
	certain to remain safe and unthreatened

seductive	2009 행정안전부 9급
	(성적으로) 유혹[매혹/고혹]적인, 마음을 끄는
	making someone do or want something, sexually attractive

segment	2014 제1회 지방직 9급, 2006 중앙인사위원회 9급
	부분, 조각
	a part of something that is different from or affected differently from the whole in some way

self–deception	2013 안전행정부
	자기기만
	Self–deception involves allowing yourself to believe something about yourself that is not true, because the truth is more unpleasant.

self–evident	2009 행정안전부 9급, 2005 대구시 9급
	자명한
	clearly true and needing no more proof

2005 중앙인사위원회 9급

self-made

자수성가한, 자력으로 성공한[출세한], 자력으로 만든, 자작의

a self-made man or woman has become successful and rich by their own efforts, not by having money given to them

2009 행정안전부 9급

self-examination

자기반성, (질병의 징후를 발견하기 위한) 자기진단

careful examination of your own behavior and beliefs to see whether they are good or bad, the act or practice of checking your body for symptoms of illness

2013 안전행정부 9급

sensible

분별 있는, 지각 있는, 상식적인, 똑똑한, 사리에 맞는

reasonable, practical, and showing good judgment

 It's _____ to keep a note of your passport number.

🔲 sensible

2013 안전행정부

sensitive

민감한, 과민한, 감각이 예민한, 여린

easily upset or offended by events or things that people say ; easily affected or damaged by something such as a substance or temperature

2005 대구시 9급

serve

~에 봉사하다, ~을 섬기다, ~을 위하여 일하다, ~에 쓸모가 있다

to give someone food or drink, especially as part of a meal or in a restaurant, bar, etc. ; to help the customers in a shop, especially by bringing them the things that they want ; to be useful or helpful for a particular purpose or reason

2012 상반기 지방직 9급

shorthand

속기, 약칭

a compendious and rapid method or writing by substituting characters, abbreviations, or symbols, for letters, words, etc.

2011 행정안전부 9급

shove

(거칠게) 밀치다[떠밀다], 아무렇게나 놓다[넣다]

to push someone or something forcefully

2012 행정안전부 9급

shoplift

가게 물건을 훔치다

the theft of goods from a shop

siege

2005 국회사무처 8급

포위, 포위 공격, 공략

a situation in which an army or the police surround a place and try to gain control of it or force someone to come out of it

sight

2013 안전행정부 9급, 2005 대구시 9급

발견하다, 찾아내다, 보다

to see something from a long distance away, or see something you have been looking for

signify

2008 행정안전부 9급

의미하다, (행동으로 감정·의도 등을) 나타내다[보여 주다], 〈보통 의문문·부정문에 쓰여〉중요하다, 문제가 되다

to be an indication of, to be of importance

significant

2013 안전행정부

중요한, 주목할 만한, ~의 뜻을 나타내는, 의미 있는

having an important effect or influence, especially on what will happen in the future ; large enough to be noticeable or have noticeable effects

sinus

2010 행정안전부 9급

부비강(두개골 속의, 코 안쪽으로 이어지는 구멍), 구멍

any of the spaces inside the head that are connected to the back of the nose

skillful

2005 대구시 9급

숙련된, 솜씨 좋은, 능숙한

good at doing something, especially something that needs special ability or training ; made or done very well, showing a lot of ability

 After a few years, he became very _____ at drawing.

📄 skillful

skim

2014 사회복지직 9급

대강 읽다, 대충 훑어보다

to read something quickly to find the main facts or ideas in it

skirmish

2008 하반기 지방직 9급

(군대의, 특히 계획에 없던) 소규모 접전[충돌], (특히 정치적 반대자들 간의) 작은 충돌[언쟁], 소규모 충돌[작은 언쟁]을 벌이다

a brief battle between small groups, a minor dispute

slight

경멸(=contempt)

an insult by showing neglect

 Example She may take it as a _____ on her ability as a mother.

📝 slight

slimy

2005 중앙인사위원회 9급

끈적끈적한, 점액성의, 불쾌한, 더러운

covered with slime, or wet and slippery like slime ; friendly in an unpleasant way that does not seem sincere — used to show disapproval

sluggish

2008 하반기 지방직 9급

느릿느릿 움직이는, 부진한

slow-moving or inactive.

smoke signal

2005 중앙인사위원회 9급

매연 신호[경보]

a message sent out to people who are far away, using the smoke from a fire, used especially by Native Americans in past times

snugly

2011 행정안전부 9급

아늑하게, 포근하게, 편안하게

providing or enjoying warmth, shelter, and comfort

sobriety

2012 상반기 지방직 9급

술에 취하지 않은 상태, 맨 정신, 냉철함, 진지함

the state of not being drunk, the quality of being serious

solely

2010 행정안전부 9급, 2006 중앙인사위원회 9급

혼자서, 단독으로, 아주, 오직

not involving anything or anyone else

solemn

2005 국회사무처 8급, 2005 대구시 9급

엄숙한, 진지한, 중대한, 격식 차린

very serious and not happy, for example because something bad has happened or because you are at an important occasion ; a solemn promise is one that is made very seriously and with no intention of breaking it ; performed in a very serious way

solicitude	2012 상반기 지방직 9급 배려 to concern that someone feels about someone's health, happiness, etc.
solitary	2017 인사혁신처, 2016 서울특별시 9급 혼자의, 단독의, 외로운(=lonely), 외딴 ; 혼자 사는 사람, 은자 used to emphasize that there is only one of something ; doing something without anyone else with you ; spending a lot of time alone, usually because you like being alone ; someone who lives completely alone
solution	2014 제1회 지방직 9급, 2005 대구시 9급 용액, 용해제 a liquid in which a solid or gas has been mixed
space shuttle	2005 국회사무처 8급 (유인) 우주 왕복선 a vehicle that is designed to go into space and return to Earth several times
specific	2015 인사혁신처 9급, 2014 제1회 지방직 9급, 2013 안전행정부 특정한, 분명한, 명확한, 구체적인 a specific thing, person, or group is one particular thing, person, or group ; detailed and exact
spiritual	2005 대구시 9급 정신의, 정신적인(↔ material) relating to your spirit rather than to your body or mind
spoil	2010 서울시 9급 망치다, 상하게 하다, (흥미·식욕 등을) 깨다, (남의) 성격[성질]을 버리다 to have a bad effect on something so that it is no longer attractive, enjoyable, useful, etc.
squeeze	2016 서울특별시 9급 쥐어짜다, 짜내다 If you squeeze something, you press it firmly, usually with your hands.
stake	2006 중앙인사위원회 9급 ~에 막대기를 세워 표시를 하다, ~을 막대기로 칸을 막다, 막대기로 둘러싸다 ; 이해관계 to mark or enclose an area of ground with stakes ; if you have a stake in a business, you have invested money in it

steady	2016 인사혁신처 9급 안정된, 꾸준한, 변함없는, 한결같은 A steady situation continues or develops gradually without any interruptions and is not likely to change quickly.
steamship	2005 중앙인사위원회 9급 (대형) 기선, 상선 a large ship that uses steam to produce power
stem	2005 국회사무처 8급 막다, 저지하다 to stop something from happening, spreading, or developing ; to stop the flow of a liquid

 The measures are meant to _____ the tide of illegal immigration.

📝 stem

stigma	2006 중앙인사위원회 9급 오명, 불명예 a strong feeling in society that being in a particular situation or having a particular illness is something to be ashamed of
stock	2014 제1차 순경, 2006 서울시 9급, 2005 중앙인사위원회 9급 혈통, 종족, 주식, 재고품, 저장 ancestry ; descent
stockholder	2006 중앙인사위원회 9급 주주 someone who owns stocks in a business
strand	2007 행정자치부 9급 (실 · 전선 · 머리카락 등의) 가닥[올/줄], (생각 · 계획 · 이야기 등의) 가닥[부분] a single thin length of thread, wire, etc., especially as twisted together with others, an element that forms part of a complex whole
strategy	2012 상반기 지방직 9급 전략, 책략 a planned series of actions for achieving something ; the skill of planning the movements of armies in a war, or an example of this

stratify	2005 국회사무처 8급 층을 이루다, (사회 등을) 계층화하다, ~을 층으로 배열하다 to classify or arrange things into different grades, levels or social classes
strengthen	2006 중앙선거관리위원회 9급 강하게 하다, 강화하다 to become stronger or make something stronger

> Example Our friendship has steadily _____ over the years.
> strengthened

stress	2015 사회복지직 9급, 2014 사회복지직 9급, 2006 서울시 9급 강조, 압박(감), 압력, 강세 the special attention or importance given to a particular idea, fact, or activity ; the physical force or pressure on an object
strict	2014 제1회 지방직 9급 엄격한, 가혹한, 엄밀한 expecting people to obey rules or to do what you say ; a strict order or rule is one that must be obeyed ; exact and correct, often in a way that seems unreasonable
strife	2012 행정안전부 9급 (개인 · 집단 간의) 갈등, 불화, (모든 종류의) 문제 violent or angry disagreement, all kinds of problems
stringent	2005 중앙인사위원회 9급 (규칙 등이) 엄격한, 엄중한, 긴급한, 자금이 핍박한, (학설 등이) 설득력이 있는 a stringent law, rule, standard, etc. is very strict and must be obeyed ; stringent economic conditions exist when there is a severe lack of money and strict controls on the supply of money
stuff	2006 서울시 9급 ~을 채워 넣다, (솜 · 털 등을) 넣다 ; 재료 to fill something until it is full ; to push or put something into a small space, especially in a quick careless way
stuffed shirt	2006 서울시 9급 격식을 차리는 사람, 젠체하는 사람 someone who behaves in a very formal way and thinks that they are important

stun

2009 상반기 지방직 9급

(특히 머리를 때려) 기절시키다, 망연자실하게 만들다, 큰 감동을 주다

to surprise or upset someone very much, to knock unconscious or into a dazed or semi-conscious state

subconscious

2001 행정자치부 9급

잠재의식적인, 어렴풋이 의식하는 ; 잠재의식

subconscious feelings, desires, etc. are hidden in your mind and affect your behavior, but you do not know that you have them ; the part of your mind that has thoughts and feelings you do not know about

suburbia

2011 행정안전부 9급

교외, 교외 풍의 생활 양식

suburbs in general, the way of life of people who live in the outer parts of a town

subliminal

2016 지방직 9급

알지 못하는 사이 영향을 미치는

Subliminal influences or messages affect your mind without you being aware of it.

subsist

2008 하반기 지방직 9급

근근이 살아가다, 존속되다, 유효하다

maintain or support oneself, especially at a minimal level, remain in being, force, or effect.

substantiality

2010 상반기 지방직 9급

실재성, 실속 있음, 본체, 견고

the state of being substantial, the extent to which something is substantial

subtlety

2010 행정안전부 9급

미묘함, 교묘함, 절묘함, 중요한 세부 요소[사항] 들

the quality or state of being subtle, a small detail that is usually important but not obvious

suicide

2006 중앙인사위원회 9급

자살

the act of killing yourself

suitable

2013 안전행정부 9급

(~에) 적당한, 상당한, 알맞은

having the right qualities for a particular person, purpose, or situation

sultry

2007 행정자치부 9급

무더운, 후텁지근한, (여성·여성의 외모가) 관능적인

uncomfortably warm and with air that is slightly wet, exciting strong sexual desire

superior	2014 제1회 지방직 9급 ~보다 위의, 보다 높은, 상급의 better, more powerful, more effective, etc. than a similar person or thing, especially one that you are competing against ; having a higher position or rank than someone else
superstition	2006 중앙인사위원회 9급 미신 a belief that some objects or actions are lucky or unlucky, or that they cause events to happen, based on old ideas of magic
supplant	2008 상반기 지방직 9급 (특히 낡거나 구식이 된 것을) 대신[대체]하다 to take the place of someone or something that is old or no longer used or accepted
survey	2013 안전행정부 조사, 답사, 개관 ; ~을 조사하다, 바라보다 an examination of an area of land in order to make a map of it ; an examination of a house or other building done especially for someone who wants to buy it ; to examine the condition of a house or other building and make a report on it, especially for people who want to buy it ; to look at or consider someone or something carefully, especially in order to form an opinion about them
susceptible	2009 행정안전부 9급 민감한, (감수성이) 예민한, ~을 허용 할 수 있는 likely to be affected by something
suspicious	2013 안전행정부 (불법 · 부정행위를 한 것으로) 의혹을 갖는, 수상쩍어 하는 If you are suspicious of someone or something, you do not trust them, and are careful when dealing with them.
swath	2009 상반기 지방직 9급 (목초 · 보리 등의) 한 번 낫질한 자취, 한 번 벤 목초, 넓은 길, 긴 행렬, (항해) 물결의 폭 a row or line of grass, corn, etc. as it falls when mown or reaped, a broad strip or area : vast swathes of land
symptom	2013 제1회 지방직 징후, 징조, 조짐, 증후, 증상 something wrong with your body or mind which shows that you have a particular illness ; a sign that a serious problem exists

	2008 상반기 지방직 9급, 2005 대구시 9급
synthetic	인조의, 합성의, 가짜의, 종합의
	produced by combining different artificial substances, rather than being naturally produced
	2005 중앙인사위원회 9급
taciturn	말 없는, 과묵한
	speaking very little, so that you seem unfriendly
	2016 지방직 9급
taint	(평판 등을) 더럽히다, 오점[오명]을 남기다
	If a person or thing is tainted by something bad or undesirable, their status or reputation is harmed because they are associated with it.
	2013 안전행정부 9급
take off	도약, 출발(점), 이륙(점)
	a starting-point ; an instance of an aircraft leaving the ground
	2010 상반기 지방직 9급
tantalizing	애타게 하는, 감질나게 하는
	to cause someone to feel interest or excitement about something that is very attractive, appealing, etc.
	2005 대구시 9급
tasty	맛 좋은, 감칠맛이 있는, 맛이 잘 든
	food that is tasty has a good taste, but is not sweet
	2006 서울시 9급
teem	충만하다, 풍부하다
	to be very full of people or animals, all moving about

 Example The island was _____ with tourists.

📖 teeming

2012 상반기 지방직 9급

temperance 절제, 절도, 자제, 절주, 금주

sensible control of the things you say and do, especially the amount of alcohol you drink ; when someone never drinks alcohol because of their moral or religious beliefs

term

말, 용어, 기간, 학기, (지불 · 요금 등의) 조건, 조항, 요금

a word or expression with a particular meaning, especially one that is used for a specific subject or type of language ; a fixed period of time during which someone does something or something happens ; one of the three periods of time that the school or university year is divided into ; the conditions that are set for an agreement, contract, arrangement, etc.

Example "Multimedia" is the _____ for any technique combining sounds and images.

term

terminal

말단, 맨끝, 종점, 종착역, (컴퓨터) 단말기, 터미널 ; 끝의, (병 등이) 말기의, 불치의

one of the points at which you can connect wires in an electrical circuit ; a piece of computer equipment consisting of at least a keyboard and a screen, that you use for putting in or taking out information from a large computer ; a big building where people wait to get onto planes, buses, or ships, or where goods are loaded ; a terminal illness cannot be cured, and causes death

the cost of living

생활비

the amount of money you need to pay for the food, clothes, etc. you need to live

the First Amendment

(美) 헌법 수정 조항 제1조(종교 · 언론 · 집회 · 청원의 자유를 보장 ; 흔히 언론의 자유 조항)

a part of the Constitution of the United States which gives US citizens the right of freedom of speech, freedom of the press(=newspapers, radio, and television), freedom of religion, and freedom of assembly(=the right of any group to meet together). Many cases concerning these rights have been taken to the Supreme Court.

thereby

그것에 의하여, 그 때문에

with the result that something else happens

		2010 상반기 지방직 9급
thesauruses	유의어 사전	
	a type of dictionary in which words with similar meanings are arranged in groups	
		2005 국회사무처 8급
thinker	사상가, 사색가	
	someone who thinks carefully about important subjects such as science or philosophy, especially someone who is famous for thinking of new ideas	
		2006 중앙인사위원회 9급
thoroughfare	통로, 도로	
	the main road through a place such as a city or village	
		2008 상반기 지방직 9급
tidbit	맛있는 가벼운 음식, (맛있는 것의) 한 입, 재미있는 이야기, 토막 뉴스	
	a small piece of tasty food, a small and particularly interesting item of gossip or information	
		2005 중앙인사위원회 9급
tincture	냄새, 기미, 약간	
	a slight flavor, trace or addition	
		2007 행정자치부 9급
top-notch	(비 격식) 최고의, 아주 뛰어난	
	of the highest quality	
		2005 중앙인사위원회 9급
transaction	처리, 취급, 거래, 교류	
	a business deal or action, such as buying or selling something ; the process of doing business	
		2005 중앙인사위원회 9급
transcontinental	대륙 횡단의, 대륙 저편의	
	crossing a continent	
		2006 서울시 9급
transcript	사본, 등본, (학교의) 성적 증명서	
	a written or printed copy of a speech, conversation, etc. ; an official college document that shows a list of a student's classes and the results they received	
		2005 대구시 9급
transient	일시의, 일시적인, 순간적인, 덧없는, 무상한	
	continuing only for a short time ; working or staying somewhere for only a short time	

tremendous	2016 인사혁신처 9급 거대한, 엄청난, 굉장한 You use tremendous to emphasize how strong a feeling or quality is, or how large an amount is.
trial	2013 안전행정부 시도, 시험, 시련, 공판, 재판 a process of testing to find out whether something works effectively and is safe ; something that is difficult to deal with, and that is worrying or annoying ; a legal process in which a judge and often a jury in a court of law examine information to decide whether someone is guilty of a crime
trigger	2013 서울시 9급 발사하다, 폭발시키다, 일으키다, 유발하다 ; 방아쇠 to make something such as a bomb or electrical system start to operate ; to make something happen very quickly, especially a series of events ; the part of a gun that you pull with your finger to fire it

Example The burglars fled after _____ the alarm.

答 triggering

2006 중앙선거관리위원회 9급

trousers

(남자용) 바지

a piece of clothing that covers the lower half of your body, with a separate part fitting over each leg

2006 행정자치부 9급

turbulent

격동의, (물·공기가) 요동을 치는, 난기류의, (사람들이) 사납게 날뛰는

moving in an irregular or violent way, full of confusion, violence, or disorder

2011 행정안전부 9급

unashamedly

염치없이

feeling or showing no guilt or embarrassment

2005 대구시 9급

unattractive

매력 없는, 남의 눈을 끌지 못하는, 애교가 없는, 따분한

not attractive, pretty, or pleasant to look at ; not good or desirable

2005 대구시 9급

unbearable

견딜 수 없는

too unpleasant, painful, or annoying to deal with

uncover	덮개를 벗기다, 뚜껑을 열다, (비밀 등을) 알아내다
	to discover something secret or hidden or remove something covering something else
underestimate	싸게 견적 내다, 과소평가하다, 얕잡아 보다, 경시하다 ; 과소평가, 경시
	to think or guess that something is smaller, cheaper, easier, etc. than it really is ; to think that someone is not as good, clever, or skilful, as they really are
undergo	겪다, 경험하다
	If you undergo something necessary or unpleasant, it happens to you.
undisturbed	방해받지 않은, 교란되지 않은, 평온한
	not interrupted or moved
unflagging	쇠하지 않는, 지칠 줄 모르는
	not decreasing or becoming weaker ; remaining strong
unhealthy	건강하지 못한, 건강에 나쁜, 위험한, 무분별한
	not physically healthy ; likely to make you ill ; not normal or natural and likely to be harmful
unnameable	이름붙일 수 없는, 말할 수 없는
	not able to be named
unprejudiced	편견이 없는, 선입관이 없는, 공평한(=impartial)
unprecedented	전례없는, 미증유의
	If something is unprecedented, it has never happened before.
unwieldy	(크기·모양·무게 때문에) 다루기 불편한[거추장스러운], (너무 크거나 복잡해서) 통제[조직]하기 힘든
	difficult to carry, manage or operate because of its size, weight or shape or complexity, badly managed, operated or moved

urbane	2006 서울시 9급
	세련된
	behaving in a relaxed and confident way in social situations
usefulness	2006 중앙선거관리위원회 9급
	유능, 쓸모 있음, 유용함
	the state of being useful or the degree to which something is useful
value	2013 제1회 지방직 9급
	(금전으로) 평가하다, 값을 매기다, 높이 평가하다, 존중하다
	to decide how much money something is worth, by comparing it with similar things ; to think that someone or something is important
variation	2013 제1회 지방직 9급
	변화(=change), 변동, 변화량, 변종, 이형
	a difference between similar things, or a change from the usual amount or form of something ; something that is done in a way that is different from the way it is usually done
vapor	2009 행정안전부 9급
	(공기 중의 수증기 · 김 · 안개 · 운무 등) 증기, 허황된 생각, 우울증
	gas or extremely small drops of liquid which result from the heating of a liquid or solid
verbal	2005 국회사무처 8급
	말의, 말에 관한, 구두의
	spoken rather than written ; relating to words or using words
verify	2012 행정안전부 9급
	(진실인지 · 정확한지) 확인하다, 입증하다
	to prove that something exists or is true, or to make certain that something is correct
versatile	2006 서울시 9급
	다재다능한
	someone who is versatile has many different skills
veteran	2010 상반기 지방직 9급
	(어떤 분야의) 베테랑, 참전 용사
	someone who fought in a war as a soldier, someone who has a lot of experience in a particular activity, job, etc

veterinary surgeon

2008 상반기 지방직 9급

(영) 수의사[= (미) veterinarian]

someone who is trained to give medical care and treatment to sick animals

veto

2005 국회사무처 8급

(거부권을 행사하여) (의안 등을) 거부하다 ; (대통령 · 지사 등의) 거부권, 거부

if someone in authority vetoes something, they refuse to allow it to happen, especially something that other people or organizations have agreed ; to refuse to accept a particular plan or suggestion ; a refusal to give official permission for something, or the right to refuse to give such permission

Example President Bush _____ the bill on July 6.

vetoed

via

2006 중앙선거관리위원회 9급

~을 경유하여, ~을 거쳐(= by way of)

traveling through a place on the way to another place

viability

2011 행정안전부 9급

(특히 태아 · 신생아의) 생육[생존] 능력, (계획 등의) 실행 가능성

capable of working successfully, the ability to live or to succeed

victim

2014 제1차 순경, 2006 서울시 9급

희생(자), 피해자

someone who has been attacked, robbed, or murdered

vigorous

2009 상반기 지방직 9급

정력적인, 원기 왕성한, 활발한, 격렬한, 강력한

using a lot of energy and strength or determination ; strong and healthy

violently

2006 서울시 9급

심하게, 격렬하게

with a lot of force in a way that is very difficult to control

visible

2005 대구시 9급

눈에 보이는, (육안으로) 볼 수 있는

something that is visible can be seen

vocational	2011 상반기 지방직 9급 **직업상의, 업무상의, 직업 교육의** teaching or relating to the skills you need to do a particular job
voluntary	2013 서울시 9급 **자발적인, 임의의, 고의의, 의도적인** voluntary work/service, etc. is work, etc. that is done by people who do it because they want to, and who are not paid ; done willingly and without being forced
vulnerable	2014 제1차 순경 **상처 입기 쉬운, 공격받기 쉬운, 비난받기 쉬운** someone who is vulnerable can be easily harmed or hurt ; a place, thing, or idea that is vulnerable is easy to attack or criticize
vulture	2005 대구시 9급 **독수리, 콘도르(주로 죽은 고기를 주식으로 하는 맹금)** a large bird that eats dead animals
waive	2005 대구시 9급 **(권리 · 주장 등을) 버리다, 포기하다, 철회하다** to state officially that a right, rule, etc. can be ignored

---

Example She _____ her right to a lawyer.

waived

---

warp	2010 행정안전부 9급 **(원래의 모습을 잃고) 휘다[틀어지다], (행동 등을) 비뚤어지게 만들다** to make or become bent or twisted out of shape, typically from the action of heat or damp
waterway	2005 중앙인사위원회 9급 **수로, 물길, 항로** a river or canal that boats travel on
wedlock	2005 국회사무처 8급 **결혼[부부] 생활, 혼인** the state of being married
welfare	2014 법원사무직 9급, 2006 중앙선거관리위원회 9급 **복지, 번영, 행복** help that is provided for people who have personal or social problems ; someone's welfare is their health and happiness

well-being
2005 국회사무처 8급

행복, 안녕, 복지

a feeling of being comfortable, healthy, and happy ; the well-being of a country is the state in which it is strong and doing well

wheezing
2009 상반기 지방직 9급

천명, 쌕쌕 거림

to breathe loudly and with difficulty

whereas
2013 안전행정부 9급

반면에, 그런데, ~에 반하여, ~이기 때문에

used to say that although something is true of one thing, it is not true of another ; used at the beginning of an official document to mean "because of a particular fact"

 Example The old system was fairly complicated _____ the new system is really very simple.

답 whereas

whimper
2012 상반기 지방직 9급

훌쩍이다, 훌쩍이며 말하다, 훌쩍거림

to make a quiet crying sound

whirlwind
2006 중앙선거관리위원회 9급

회오리바람, (감정의) 폭풍

an extremely strong wind that moves quickly with a circular movement, causing a lot of damage

wholeheartedly
2011 행정안전부 9급

진심으로, 착실하게, 진정으로, 전적으로

having or showing no doubt or uncertainty about doing something, supporting someone, etc.

wildlife
2006 중앙인사위원회 9급

야생 생물

animals and plants growing in natural conditions

wire
2006 중앙선거관리위원회 9급

배선을 설치하다, 전선을 가설하다

to connect wires inside a building or piece of equipment so that electricity can pass through ; to connect electrical equipment to the electrical system using wires

2005년부터 2019년까지 국가직·지방직 등 공무원시험에서 출제되었던 기출숙어의 의미를
정리하여 단어뿐만 아니라 효율적인 숙어학습이 가능하도록 구성하였습니다.
빈칸 채우기를 통해 완성된 문장을 만들면서 숙어의 의미를 다시 한 번 확인할 수 있습니다.